RE-ENSOULING EDUCATION

ESSAYS ON THE IMPORTANCE OF THE HUMANITIES IN SCHOOLING THE SOUL

edited by
Dennis Patrick Slattery
and
Jennifer Leigh Selig
with
Stephen A. Aizenstat

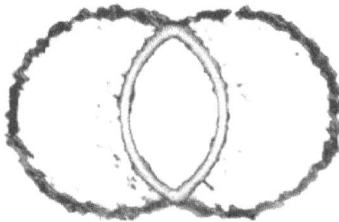

MANDORLA BOOKS

ISBN: 978-1-950186-03-7

Previously released as *The Soul Does Not Specialize: Revaluing the Humanities and the Polyvalent Imagination* (2012)

Designed by Jennifer Leigh Selig

Cover art by Tallmadge Doyle
"Kepler's Cosmic Geometry XII"
www.tallmadgedoyle.com
Used with permission.

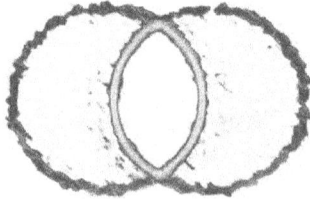

MANDORLA BOOKS
WWW.MANDORLABOOKS.COM

In our undertaking of fostering an event of *communitas*, we devote our study to texts that bear the increment of many minds, many cultures, many myths. Thus, through reading, writing listening, and discussing, members of this group are given the opportunity to redefine themselves in a moral cosmos larger than any one culture could provide. In this context they can come to understand the roots of their separate commitments and so reconceive the roles they play in society and the callings they serve.

~**Louise Cowan,** *Classic Texts and the Nature of Authority*

The school should always have as its aim that the young person leave it as a harmonious personality, not as a specialist. Otherwise, he—with his specialized knowledge—more closely resembles a well-trained dog than a harmoniously developed person.

~**Albert Einstein,** *Out of My Later Years*

DEDICATION

To every teacher in my life and in the lives of every student, who incited a spark of wonder, a hunger for learning and the joy that emanated from between the two.

~Dennis Patrick Slattery

To Dennis and Steve, ever your student, ever and beyond blessed.

~Jennifer Leigh Selig

To remembering the humanity of every child and adult left behind, may their yearning for story not go untold.

~Stephen A. Aizenstat

TABLE OF CONTENTS

PREFACE TO THE 2019 EDITION

It is a pleasure to be working with my coeditors, Jennifer Selig and Stephen A. Aizenstat on the reissue of our earlier book, *The Soul Does Not Specialize: Revaluing the Humanities and the Polyvalent Imagination.* Since its original publication in 2012, the Humanities and Liberal Arts Education have been attacked with greater zeal than before, as if there were secrets in these disciplines that should not be revealed to the population at large. Sure there are! I don't want to point to the tired cliché that humanities education hones one's skills in critical thinking and discernment. It is too reductive a view of what the Humanities offer the soul of the world through the soul of its students. I have felt that pointing to critical thinking skills sounds like an apology for existing and that if those who purport to adhere to the values of a liberal education can offer a practical, useful reason for studying these disciplines, then they will be more readily accepted. Nonsense. No apologies for Humanities learning. No timid affirmation of the imagination's power to shape and cohere not only an individual life but that of an entire people.

In her book, *The Field: The Quest for the Secret Force of the Universe*, reporter Lynn McTaggart begins by showing the terms under which the world has been understood through the visions of Isaac Newton, Charles Darwin and Rene Descartes. Their voices almost exclusively set the terms of how we should understand the created order: everything and everyone is separate, distinct, autonomous; the world "is random, predatory, purposeless and solitary," she writes in her Prologue. "Life is not about sharing and interdependence" (xiv).

Not until the discoveries of quantum physics did it dawn on the scientific community, then spread from there, that another paradigm was gaining traction, one which religious and earlier native traditions had already discovered. That the tiniest pieces of matter were not what they seemed, that much of the created order had no meaning in isolation but only in relationship to one another, and that the universe was closer in attitude to "a dynamic web of interconnection. Things once in contact remained always in contact through all space and all time" (xv).

I mention this major change in world views, although the Newtonian, Cartesian and Darwinian worlds are still very much with us (though with shudders and cracks appearing throughout) because the quantum world is closer to what the Humanities offer us: a sense of relatedness of part to part and parts to whole. Essentially Humanistic studies is a (re)new(ed) myth that requires a shift from a world view of independence to one of interdependence, even though the power of tribalism today, which feeds off of us/them, seems to be gaining a stronger foothold at a historical moment when the Humanities are under assault.

A different, more holistic, interdependent, interconnected and multi-relational way of imagining is nonetheless revealing its virtues and venues for a greater level of consciousness between humans and the rest of the created order. At no time is a study of Humanistic disciplines more necessary to fully and effectively address the climates of change that run from the earth herself to the attitudes that keep us separate, divided and contesting for the top rungs of power.

The perceptive and powerful essays in this volume are qualitative, quantum ways of viewing the Humanities as avenues to connectivity and mutual accord. Think, reader, of this volume as a survival manual for the species; nothing short of that vision is necessary for our communal survival.

Dennis Patrick Slattery, Ph.D.
Faculty Emeritus, Pacifica Graduate Institute

REFERENCES

Lynn Taggart, *The Field: The Quest for the Secret Force of the Universe*. New York: Harper Perennial, 2008.

FOREWORD

There is no greater challenge facing education today then the need to reintroduce the humanities back into the classroom and into lives of our students. Our kids know that the world they live in is at great risk. Within their lifetime, climate change alone threatens their survival. The brilliance of the scientific mind, as trained by an all-too-pervasive math/science curriculum, nonetheless falls short of meeting the ensuing crisis at hand. The innovative intelligence required now lives in the depths of the human soul. To reawaken the potency and expansive range of our children's creative passion, an innate desire buried too often beneath denial and helplessness, is to again sink the tap-root of learning into the most profound source of inspiration known to human kind—the well spring of our genius, a humanities-based education.

Connecting to the psyche of nature, the creative arts, the wisdom stories of our ancestors, and to the mythic imagination opens the way to such learning. The humanities muses into vital life the intellectual and experiential attunement needed to boldly engage the world's unrelenting manic complexity being faced by our jeopardized young, one of the most imperiled generations in history.

The authors in this collection of essays, all affiliated with Pacifica Graduate Institute where I am Founding President and Chancellor, give voice to the need for a turn from the trajectory that we are on, the "science" of education (with its emphasis on accountability, teaching to the test, learning outcomes, and uniform assessment that emphasize the quantitative fantasy) to another mode of teaching/learning—the "art" of education (cultivating the imagination, opening deep curiosity, training in modes of perception and seeing with an aesthetic eye).

On a personal level, I know this turn toward a humanities-oriented education. As a freshman at UCLA, I was taken aside and "coached" by a graduate teaching assistant who was overseeing the science lab that was part of my pre-med sequence of courses. We were dissecting animal brains at the time by learning what areas of the "mind" influenced behavior. One day he asked me to put down my surgical instruments and walk with him out into the hallway. "Steve, look around; do you see anybody else in here that thinks about things the same way as you?" I never stopped to consider that idea. I was here at college, doing what I was programmed to do by parents and cultural expectations. I was taking classes in the science buildings, studying all day and night, learning mechanistically how the human body works. Seeing my depressed mood and, frankly, not very keen technique, I was encouraged to visit the "other side of campus," the North Campus, home of the Liberal Arts. At the time, I did not even know there was such a place, so immersed was I in what I was concentrating on: the scientific focus I had adopted.

My eyes could not believe what greeted me on North Campus: students sitting under the canopies of trees or in the sculpture gardens studying philosophy, contemplating the deeper meanings of life, debating the ideas behind the politics of the day, as well as passionately exploring the far reaches of imagination and consciousness. It was as if I had escaped a form of "lock down." I was liberated. Here on the North Campus, college credit was given for courses in film studies, music, art, philosophy, even political philosophy, and literature. No longer feeling isolated and dim, I joined right in. I felt something long dormant ignite and come to life within me. Once sparked, another kind of intelligence opened and offered itself to me and to those whom I was in spirited conversation and even communion. I felt a homecoming to a way of knowing, a way of being, long forgotten, having been virtually trained out of me in high school and freshman year of college by a program of study centered on causal thinking and reductive reasoning. Oh what joy to come home to the generative field of the Humanities and to the life spring bubbling under the veil of the expected.

Years later, when teaching junior and senior high school students in Santa Monica, I never forgot how that walk to North Campus had changed my life. Studies in the liberal arts evoked my curiosity and became a portal into the deeper realms of my creative and emotional intelligence. It opened the portal to what James Hillman describes as the "Blood Soul," the realm of mythic imagination and dream. While teaching in the public schools, it was not lost on me that most students go numb when faced with information-based curricula that culminate in an accountability test that asked them to choose the right answer from a, b, c, or d. Beyond rational thinking there is the yearning for expression, for imaginative meandering, for story, and for embodied experience, and these, I suggest, are the essential loam from which innate intelligence sprouts. Separated from this ground of being, both the engineer and the artist, the crafts person and philosopher suffer. All lose connection with their authentic calling, their true nature, and more importantly, their desire to participate in the joyous excitement of a fuller form of creative learning. Cultivating the humanities in education, I came to understand, enlivens psychic depth and sustains the life force, thus satisfying a medicinal need for body and soul. Pulling the Liberal Arts curriculum out by the roots from education extinguishes the yearning to dream into the not-yet-known, a form of bad medicine for what lives most importantly at the core of our being, and, in fact, "leaves most children left behind."

After leaving the world of teaching in the public schools, I found myself in the college town of Isla Vista in Santa Barbara, working on a graduate degree in Education and Psychology at the University of California. Offered the opportunity to help develop an alternative high school in Santa Monica and a middle school in Santa Barbara as part of my graduate studies, I dedicated over a decade to developing curricula that included cognitive, affective, and imaginative elements, a confluence made possible by evolving each lesson plan from the humanities. When teaching history, I offered not only time-lines and historical facts, but also readings of poets and novelists responding to the events of their times. Companioning these modern writers with epic stories from the Greek classics both opened imagination and stimulated a curiosity at deeper dimensions of human behavior and experience.

Achilles, the hero of the Trojan War, brought home the agony and the ecstasy of the timeless struggles and sufferings of loss always present in the actuality of human conflict. In English classes as well, studies engaged more than reading a text and writing an essay or answering a set of multiple-choice questions. The classroom came alive as students worked imaginatively, for example in enacting scenes from the narrative, opening body, mind, and soul, as they creatively entered the material and moved from mental memorization to enlivened expression. The humanities brought the animated psyche as well as the activity of soul into the learning process. Teaching and learning became an artistic practice, a craft, and not simply an exercise of training the rational mind.

At the time I was teaching in the public schools, with the help of an initial seed grant from the University of California Regents, I co-founded a counseling center in Isla Vista, later to evolve into Pacifica Graduate Institute. With modest beginnings and offering two degrees, Pacifica has grown today to offer graduate degrees with multiple specializations in Depth Psychology, Mythological Studies, and Engaged Humanities. From its inception, what set and continues to set Pacifica apart as a graduate school is the unwavering conviction that the pervasive inclusion of the humanities in curricula awakens the best and most interdisciplinary of academic studies. Research at Pacifica, both qualitative and quantitative, originates in the "calling" of the student, in the "soul spark" of an idea, found in the inner landscapes of the whole person. Cultivated over the years by ongoing studies of the humanities, we have witnessed a quality of consciousness emerge. For example, in psychology, the *Diagnostic and Statistical Manual* is taught both as an esteemed map for making differential diagnosis and as a document to include the mythological underpinnings that speak to the pathos of the human experience.

An education of and in-depth, which serves as a common ground for Pacifica's programs, opens imagination, stimulates creative thinking, and elaborates on the "poetic basis" of mind. A thoughtful reading, for example, of Shakespeare or Dante deepens the understanding of the human condition as much as analyzing the results of the latest clinical trials or the newest theory of personality. As psychology is informed by the mythological imagination, so too is the field of Mythological Studies informed by a psychology of depth. Both are enhanced by the universal stories, epic poetry, and the creative arts. This educational formulation creates the juice, the distinction, the ever-present vision that guides graduate work at Pacifica. The mission of the institute is informed by its motto *"animae mundi colendae gratia"*—for the sake of tending the soul of and in the world. An education based in the humanities constellates more than a course of study; it mobilizes the learning community around an advocacy, a commitment intended to take the richly textured imaginative capacities of the human experience into every facet of community life and culture.

It is no accident that what lives at the bottom of our unique interdisciplinary approach to soul-centered education is the dream. The multifarious expressions of the dreaming process offer in visible ways the figures of imagination who in turn, when tended, muse our work. These figures offer insight and inspiration, and above all, they carry with them an innate intelligence, often unrealized in conscious awareness. Like a fully-formed character in a play or a great novel, these figures of the dreamtime have an intelligence of their own, interrelating with one another along with us. They impact our behavior and mood, create afflictions and inspiration, and some would even say are "those" responsible, from the beginning, for the way we act and how we live our life (first image, then behavior). In dreams the drama continues night after night, even occurring during the daylight hours as waking dreams. The inner story, the plot or mythos of our life, is carried by these figures. At Pacifica, tending to the visitants of the dream world comprises an important part of our curriculum. An education in the humanities cannot leave out this inner narrative. From our point of view, not only are the voices of our personal experience and our shared cultural archetypal backgrounds expressed in dreams, but the creatures, landscapes, and things of the world also make their appearance as dream images in the inscape of dreaming. Our relationship to the humanities becomes more than human-centered. In addition, it includes the "others," with whom we co-exist on the planet.

Attending to dream life animates our modes of perception, as we develop new ways of seeing and listening to their activities, feelings, their intentions. As we bring a "witnessing presence" to their presentation, we feel the claim being made on our experience. And then something quite extraordinary happens: no longer do we feel trapped in the manic world of commerce, or the rational realm of causal thought, or even what sometimes feels like the prison of expectations, our own or that which others have in mind for us. Indeed, we are liberated, if only for a time, to be a participant in a drama bigger then what is familiar and habitual; we discover ourselves anew in the poetics of the dream, alive and interactive with the images of the animated soul.

If I have learned anything in my career as a classroom teacher, a founder of a graduate institute, a professor, a dream worker, it is this: an education in the humanities and an on-going relationship with dream life opens imagination and offers what science alone cannot—access to the very source of innovation and creativity. What the world is requesting of us, indeed, what industry and government are asking, what the species (ours and so many others) is demanding from us now, is the rediscovery of an innate intelligence alive in the world behind the visible world. Activating imagination through an enlivened relationship with the depths of our humanity opens the door, points the way, and values what we have always known to be true and that which we hold dear: a life blessed with the abundance of beauty and the smile of Aphrodite in all that we encounter.

Stephen A. Aizenstat, Ph.D.
Founder and Chancellor of Pacifica Graduate Institute

INTRODUCTION

HUMANITIES EDUCATION:
NECESSITIES FOR CULTIVATING THE WHOLE PERSON

Not so long ago I was with my granddaughter, aged ten at the time. We were returning from seeing the film, *Despicable Me* together and were talking about the parts we each liked the most. As we discussed the film driving home, and as the mystery of conversing with an astute ten year old can turn, we began to speak of mythology, especially the Greek stories of gods, goddesses and mortals. I remarked that I liked the myths very much, especially the story of Demeter and Persephone. At that, McKenzie began to relate the story to me and was excited about the pomegranate that Demeter, now held by Hades in the underworld, ate, thus insuring that part of every year would be spent in this nether region. She found the fruit wonderful and felt it was the primary part of the story.

I was surprised by this story as well as others that she began to relate: of the three brothers, Zeus, Poseidon and Hades and of what made the middle brother so perpetually angry and discontented, or the uneasy marriage between Zeus and Hera, and the powerful beauty of Athena. As she relayed one set of figures after another, I finally interrupted and told her: how great that you attend a public school in San Antonio and they teach mythology. Of that idea I was quickly corrected. "No papa," she responded, "they don't teach mythology to us. I go to the library and check out books on Greek myths because I love the stories." "You taught yourself these stories?" I asked. "Yes," was her reply. At that moment I resolved to buy her as many books on Greek myth as she could handle and have done so since.

This young lady is also an Honors Student in Math and Science studies as well; she fully enjoys a special privilege three times a week of having class upstairs in a seminar arrangement where she and seven other students from multiple grade levels converse broadly across several disciplines. I cannot applaud her public school enough for accelerating the learning in their program through conversation that spans both arts and sciences. McKenzie is a student of the humanities; her seminars reveal to her and others the interconnections between disciplines of study and help them discern relationships between the sciences and the humanities. She loves it and waits for those three times per week to play with ideas with like-talented students.

In our trip home I marveled at her natural desire to know and to know broadly. She checked out the books on mythology because her appetite to know about these mysterious and wondrous characters could be satisfied in no other way. I suspect as well that, given her gift to express herself so well at such a young age, that she also loves words, language, and their power in conversation to shape ideas, opinions and worlds of meaning.

Under the growing mechanistic model of learning, the humanities are being assaulted as unnecessary and often superfluous arenas of study for they do not necessarily, the thinking goes, lead to job procurement and financial security. Underneath this thinking roils the myth of capitalism, which fundamentally reduces everything it brushes against into a commodity to be purchased or a price tag to reflect value. Direct cause-to-effect formatting places all learning on the procrustean bed of efficiency and job acquisition and dismembers the rest as irrelevant. The danger here is that the myth that guides such thinking, both capitalistic and corporate, is strong enough to dissolve an entire culture, and by extension, civilization. Such is the power of the myth that extols learning as a way into job procurement. If all learning has such a goal, than yes, humanities education has no part in the process and as a consequence both the individual and culture at large are de-humanized. The totality of the human is lost as the humanities are subverted.

In his Introduction to a fine collection of essays, *What's Happened to the Humanities?* editor Alvin Kernan notes that "Historically, the humanities are the old subjects, which in many forms and under a variety of names—the nine muses; the liberal arts; quadrivium and trivium; rhetoric, dialectic, and logic; humane letters—were the major part of Western education for over two millennia (3). Today, funding is being carved from the National Endowment for the Humanities study programs, which are dismissed by the corporate model as just another entitlement that we must downgrade or eliminate in the service of "fiscal responsibility." Recently, in the state where I reside, a legislature in the Austin capital in Texas went so far as to call public education itself "another entitlement program that needs to be trimmed back." To do so is to assassinate history itself and with it, the tradition that we have grown out of as well as others that have helped to shape our own. Such is one of humanities' tasks: to keep history itself alive and relevant.

Not surprisingly, Texas ranks at the bottom of the national education ladder as a state in which the highest number of adults without a high school degree reside; furthermore, it holds the title as a state with one of the lowest expenditures for students in public education. In the years 2011-2012 Texas will spend $800.00 less per student for public learning. These figures are symptomatic of the disdain that some feel towards learning generally as a useless activity if it is not job-acquisition leaning. Texas, of course, is not the only state eviscerating its public education budget. What has dropped out of the public discussion in large measure is the intrinsic value of the humanities for the health and vitality of a culture. The essays in this volume wish to address, each in its own manner, what value such learning can have on the texture of a people's imagination, and, by extension, the degree and quality of a people's liberty as self-determined rather than reduced to manipulated hordes.

BRAVE NEW WORLD IS NOW

In a recent interview in *The Progressive,* journalist and senior fellow at the Nation Institute, Chris Hedges offers a sobering assessment of the news media, the two party system and the corporate take-over of United States governance. In the course of the interview Hedges admits: "I used to wonder: Is Huxley right or is Orwell right? It turns out they're both right" (*The Progressive,* 35). Both *Brave New World* and *1984* might with great reward be retrieved as essential reading for anyone interested in challenging the assaults on the humanities and, more generally, on learning itself. Both novels can be found today even in airport bookstores, so ubiquitous are these texts today, decades after their initial publication. Their easy availability is no accident. My interest here, however, is to address only Huxley's dystopic vision.

In his Foreword to a relatively new edition of *Brave New World,* cultural critic Christopher Hitchens notes that "Huxley was composing *Brave New World* at a time when modernism as we know it was just coming into full view" [1931] (Foreword xiv). The question Hitchens suggests Huxley proposed in his allegory was a simple one: "Can the human being be designed and controlled from uterus to grave 'for its own good'? And would this version of super-utilitarianism bring real happiness?" (xiv).

Within the Central London Hatchery and Conditioning Centre which holds aloft its motto: COMMUNITY, IDENTITY, STABILITY (*Brave New*

World 15), the Director of this central office points proudly to the techniques in which infants are conditioned at an early age to recoil from books and flowers. These two images are metonymies for learning and for the order of nature. Connections with learning and with the natural order are enemies to the state's desire to control all its citizens. Inside the INFANT NURSERIES, NEO-PAVOLVIAN CONDITIONING ROOMS (28) the director is delighted to demonstrate to the uninitiated the successful conditioning of 8 month olds: "all exactly alike (a Bokanovsky Group, it was evident" (29).

Initially, all of the infants are placed together on the floor. Shortly thereafter, flowers and books are placed in their vicinity. Immediately attracted by the bright colors and shapes, the infants begin eagerly to crawl towards them. They begin to play with the flowers and crumple the pages of the books. The director waits for a few moments, and then signals the conditioning process to begin as the infants delight in their play. He nods to a nurse, who throws a switch that unleashes a violent explosion of horrifying sound. "Shriller and ever shriller, a siren shrieked. Alarm bells maddeningly sounded. The children started, screamed, their faces were distorted with terror" (29). Then phase two: an electric shock is sent through the floor the infants are playing on: "Their little bodies twitched and stiffened; their limbs moved jerkily as if to the tug of unseen wires" (30).

After the power is turned off and the infants cease their terrified crying, the Director tells his nurse to "Offer them the flowers and the books again" (30). When she approaches the infants with these objects a second time, they recoil in horror; the Director proudly yawls that "what man has joined, nature is powerless to put asunder" (30). This treatment will be repeated some 200 times, which will seal what the Director has blueprinted: "They'll grow up with what the psychologists used to call an 'instinctive' hatred of books and flowers . . . . They'll be safe from books and flowers all their lives" (30). The conditioning here is based on two tropes: the book, symbol of learning through reading, contemplation, discussion and thought; the flower as symbol of the natural order, aesthetics, wildness, the untamed part of nature which promotes pleasure through escape from the city, and into the openness of the world's body. Replacing these are constant conditionings while one sleeps, including clichés that repeat their pseudo-truths ten thousand times as one is growing up in the *Brave New World*, so that all conditioning has one end: to increase consumption (38). Thought disappears and programmed responses fill in the gaps where the imagination once held a more prominent, persuasive and civilizing presence.

The leading deity adopted by this new world is Henry Ford, whose proclamation "History is bunk" assumes the mantra of the new society. Replacing history, human memory, and the standards bequeathed future generations by tradition through ancestor wisdom, are drugs that offer instant nirvana, sexual experimentation with others in casual relationships and diversions in abundance to keep the mind and body occupied and thought-less. The individual commits to nothing but distracted self-gratification. The head Controller of Western Europe as well as the program to eliminate cultural memory from the population—his ford-ship, Mustafa Mond—repeats slowly for all: *History is bunk*. As he repeats this mantra to the students he addresses, "he waved his hand, and it seemed that "with an invisible feather whisk, he had brushed away the dust of history, covered with spider webs, and the webs consisted of Thebes and Babylon and Cnossos and Mycenae":

> Whisk, Whisk—and where was Odysseus, where was Job, where were Jupiter and Gotama and Jesus? Whisk—and those specks of antique dirt called Athens and Rome, Jerusalem and the Middle Kingdom—all were gone. Whisk—the place where Italy had been was empty. Whisk, the cathedrals; whisk, whisk, King Lear and the Thoughts of Pascal. Whisk, Passion; whisk, Requ*iem; whisk,* Symphony; whisk . . . (41)

To erase the past, tradition, cultural and world histories, is effectively to assassinate the Humanities in the Brave New World, ironically a line stolen from Shakespeare's last play, *The Tempest*. Abolished in this new world is the presence of individual meaning that is outside what the state mandates as the purpose of life. Repetition of thought content heard in one's sleep over 62 thousand times erases all individual thought with "hypnopaedic proverbs" like: "Everyone belongs to every one else" (46) and "Ending is better than mending" (55) or "you can't consume much if you sit still and read books" (55). Passivity, indifference, manipulation, diversion, distraction, seeking bodily pleasures and passions all comprise the formidable terms of the new society. Huxley's allegory of a state of passive indifference through the voice of the corporate state is the final consequence of a populace that has lost the virtues of learning, inquisitiveness, wonder, philosophizing and a broad-based humanities education that promotes reflection, discernment, taste and freshly-languaged articulations of the ailments attendant on human destiny and choice. The price tag is one's complete abdication of liberty on all levels, replaced efficiently by its more trivialized version: choice of commodities and entertainments to further enforce a life of distraction.

Before turning to an alternative to such an infernal world view, one which could be argued we are fast approaching in Western culture today, I want to mention a chapter from the Canadian cultural historian, Jane Jacobs, whose classic *The Death and Life of Great American Cities* is as relevant now as when she wrote it decades ago. Her last book, *Dark Age Ahead,* [1] published in 2004 before her death, and one which opens with the line: "this is both a gloomy and a hopeful book" (3), contains a chapter entitled "Credentialing Versus Educating" (44-63).

Arguing that a degree and an education are not necessarily synonymous" (44), Jacobs asserts and then argues effectively for her thesis that "Credentialing, not educating, has become the primary business of North American universities" (44). She tracks this move to the turbulent 1960s when students, sensing a change in the quality of education they were receiving, began to complain that they had expected "more personal rapport with teachers who had become only remote figures in large, impersonal lecture halls." They also felt short-changed by professors who attempted to transmit culture "that omitted acquaintance with personal examples and failed to place them on speaking terms with wisdom" (47). These students sensed a sea change in the delivery system of learning; administrators, on the other hand were concentrating on "applying lessons from profit-making enterprises that turn expanded markets to advantage by cutting costs" because their interests resided in "increased output of product [which] can be measured more easily as numbers . . . " (49). Much of education had been seduced and consumed by the corporate model, itself a tumorous outgrowth of the scientific mechanistic model. Students were now numerically interchangeable while learning as an act of imaginative inquiry, was on all fronts now to be measured along the well-grooved route of standardized tests. Mechanization had indeed taken command.

Jacobs goes on to delineate how in the 1960s the purpose of education began to be recalculated for credentialing that would lead to job security and financial safety. Job acquisition became the purpose of all learning; what did not promote a salaried position was deemed irrelevant. Damage to the environment, mass consumption of natural resources, even war itself, were seen as job-creating enterprises and thus must heel under the banner of more people working: "To this day, no alternative disaster, including possible global warming, is deemed as dire a threat as job loss" (60). This icon of industry—the impulse in education to promote its most important purpose, credentialing as the only relevant element in cultural continuity— appears to be more prevalent today than when she made this observation seven years ago.

In the process of making credentialing the most important work of institutions of higher learning in the 60s, Jacobs observes, the good students lamented being treated as raw material to be moved through the system to graduation as quickly as possible, which often meant dropping electives that included humanities courses that one wished to study for the sheer joy of learning. The other attitude of students, to the chagrin of passionate teachers, was indifference to anything said or studied that did not directly feed the appetite of credentials, hence their work in the classroom and outside in assignments was minimal and lethargic (62). It is not difficult to discern the short line between Huxley's 1931 observations and Jacobs' some 75 years later. The pattern is clear in history, as is the imagination that develops such an austere education whose one purpose is training for a job. What is sacrificed in such a narrow corridor is cultural memory as well as discussion of the deepest problems that affect us as human beings. Along with such a paring to the bones is the squelching of a sense of wonder about how things were and are.

HUMANITIES AND THE REVIVAL OF LEARNING

The disciplines that comprise the humanities might be viewed on one level as multiple ways of remembering the traditions of thought that history reveals. To recall the wisdom of the past, to rework these mythologies that gave rise to earlier civilizations and cultures, to see ourselves in light of what has been discovered—all these can be beneficial to an intelligent and vigorous work force. To lose the points of view as ways of imagining and knowing that the humanities offer the thoughtful person is to lose our collective cultural identity. Without it, we free-float and free-fall as a people because our common heritage is sabotaged; we become victims of any propaganda that assaults us, as with the repeated clichés that invaded the sleep of people in Huxley's programmed world.

But if we stopped at simply assessing the loss of content that the humanities gift us with, we would have failed to tap into the deeper level of its intrinsic value, for the humanities offers us a particular way of being present to knowing. As early as 1980 in a report formulated by "The Commission on the Humanities," there was concern about this cluster of studies' future and offered a succinct statement of its value: "Through the humanities we reflect on the fundamental question: what does it mean to be human? The humanities offer clues but never a complete answer" (1). The report goes on to suggest that "They [the humanities] reveal how people have tried to make moral, spiritual and intellectual sense of a world in which irrationality, despair, loneliness, and death are as conspicuous as birth, friendship, hope and reason" (1).

The humanities explore, each in its varied language and method, the place of paradox, mystery, contradiction through the particular and unique turn of mind, which is always "toward history, the record of what has moved men and women before us to act, believe, and build as they did" (3).These ideas outlined by the Commission are what I wish to cultivate in my last observation.

In his now classic text, *Leisure: The Basis of Culture*, Josef Pieper, a German philosopher and theologian, argued in 1948 Germany for a way of knowing that allows time, reflection, and musing which can promote a deeper knowing. Part of his book's intention, retranslated in 1998, is to retrieve some of the ancient ideas about knowing that bear directly on the essays contained in this volume.

Early in his discussion, Pieper retrieves a dual way of knowing practiced by both ancient and medieval philosophy. He observes that the medievals "distinguished between the intellect as *ratio* and the intellect as *intellectus*" (11). The former is "the power of discursive thought, or searching and researching, abstracting, refining and concluding" (11). By contrast, *intellectus* "refers to the ability of 'simply looking' (*simplex intuitus*), to which the truth presents itself as a landscape presents itself to the eye." Both forms of cognition are necessary to satisfy what the ancients believed constituted "the spiritual knowing power of the human mind . . . . All knowing involves both" (11). *Intellectus* is more conducive to receiving, to waiting in openness, "a receptively operating power of the intellect" (12). This latter way of conceiving knowledge is closer to contemplation, a disposition that is non-aggressive, non-manipulating, and less bent on explanation; instead it is more porous and patient, willing to see what wishes to be revealed. I believe it is a form of being present that the humanities cultivate most effectively, as a disciplined way of being receptive and open, not in charge and not always guiding the reins of the intellect. Nor are the humanities seeking a definitive answer to complex questions; its instinct is not to simplify and so control.

In fact, as Pieper develops the distinction between the low "canopy" of the work world and the more transcendent canopy-breaking of liberal learning, he suggests that "the Philosopher is akin to the Poet; both are concerned with the *mirandum*—'the wondrous', the astonishing or whatever calls for astonishing, or wonder" (69). In the work world such activity is useless and irrelevant; in the world of total work "all the various forms and methods of transcendence must themselves become sterile . . ." (69). It is my belief that the essays present in this volume will each reveal how the humanities promote the philosophic and poetic act of wondering, which is the beginning impulse to philosophizing.

POETIC KNOWLEDGE AND THE RECOVERY OF EDUCATION

In his far-reaching and deeply historical work, *Poetic Knowledge: The Recovery of Education*, teacher and literary historian James Taylor crafts a persuasive case for retrieving this form of knowing. He is quick, however, to point out that poetic knowledge is not concerned with the wisdom that poetry affords us, but rather with a certain attitude towards learning that I have been developing up to this point. For this mode of knowledge is what the humanities foster, each in its own way of perceiving and interpreting the world. Taylor reveals early on what qualities comprise poetic knowing: it is intuitive; it is comfortable with obscurity and not with the fast and fixed; it allows the seen and the unseen to emerge in a unity; it cultivates the imagination, intuition, emotions and silences; it is based on a philosophical intuition; it is "a poetic (a sensory-emotional experience of reality"; it is non-analytical (5-6). Thus, poetic knowing "makes present a sensate knowing" (5) wherein the embodied person contemplating such a form of knowledge is not dis-incarnated but fully present "connaturally."

This last term, *connatural,* Taylor retrieves from the writings of St. Thomas Aquinas and, more currently from its further development by the philosopher, Jacques Maritain to designate a stance or an attitude towards knowing that I am arguing is at the heart of humanities learning: "To be connatural with a thing is to participate in some way with its nature, as distinct from its intentional form, to share a likeness of nature" (64). It is one of the central modes that leads to right judgment. Discernment, taste, right order, a sense of the relation of parts to parts and to a greater whole are all contained in connatural knowing, which stems from, according to Taylor, "all unpremeditated intellectual acts of knowing" (65). In the process, within humanities learning or knowing, one grasps that facts are insufficient; rather, the humanities is more a gathering of a world view that opens the mind to historicity itself in its profound and often perplexing continuity.

Jacques Maritain designates this attitude or stance a *habitus,* a term he pulls from the history of the ancients to express what he calls "the qualities of a class apart, qualities which are essentially stable dispositions, perfecting in the line of its own nature the subject in which they exist." So for example, he suggests that "Health, beauty are *habitus* of the body; sanctifying grace is a *habitus* (supernatural) of the soul" (10). My sense is that humanities study can have as one of its ends the development of an "operative habitus" (11) wherein the contemplation of the disciplines that comprise its terrain can lead to action, to the promotion of social justice, to a sense of authentic liberty, and to a desire to promote balance and fairness and a sense of fairness in the world.

To lose humanities education is to forfeit our collective moorings, our anchors and our sense of being placed in a world with a history and a future. Humanities education is one of imagination and vision, a means of seeing both panoramically and scenically; it develops "not simply an alert mind but an overall alertness of keen senses.... It is the habit of noticing what is happening here and now and reflecting with the natural powers upon that experience that cultivates the connatural degree of knowledge"(64-65). For my purposes, I believe *humanities knowing* begins in both trust and wonder and ends in love and respect for all that was, is and will be.

Finally, I offer the following reflections on humanities education:

- It is interdisciplinary in nature
- It is complex, subtle and consonant with the disciplines that comprise its rich field as well as the created order in all its imperfections
- It cultivates integrity
- It grounds the person and the collective in place by making one feel at home in the world
- It promotes a sense of authentic freedom
- It places us in contact directly or analogically with the world's large universal and sustaining symbols
- It guides one towards the inner truth of things
- It serves as a compass for suffering humanity
- It aids one in recognizing the larger essential patterns and energies that govern human and natural existence
- It promotes care and compassion for self and others as well as the planet in its complex entirety
- It points one to the large realm of the invisibles
- It serves as a critique or caution to excess, to appetites out of control
- It is not a method for explanation but more a willingness to be in the face of mystery and at ease, for there is always more to realize
- It promotes a sense of wonder
- It develops a habit of mind that can be transferred to any study in life and to a life lived in its fullest comprehension and satisfaction

- It fosters or makes present a sense of caution in the present by redeeming and recollecting the past so as not to duplicate its malfunctions in the present or future
- It allows us space to forgive ourselves and others by outlining the imperfect nature of being and becoming
- It reveals the paradox of unity within diversity
- It opens us to the mythic and psychic substructure of the seen world
- It brings joy and a sense of spaciousness to the one studying because one is now in touch with forces and energies far transcending the self

Dennis Patrick Slattery, Ph.D.
Core Faculty, Mythological Studies

REFERENCES

Commission on the Humanities. *Report of the Commission on the Humanities: The Humanities in American Life*. Berkeley: U of California Press, 1980.

Hedges, Chris. "The Progressive Interview." *The Progressive* 75.8 (2011): 33-37.

Hitchens, Christopher. "Foreword." *Brave New World and Brave New World Revisited*. New York: HarperPerennial, 2004. vii-xxi.

Huxley, Aldous. *Brave New World and Brave New World Revisited*. New York: HarperPerennial, 2004.

Kernan, Alvin, ed. *What's Happened to the Humanities?* Princeton: Princeton UP, 1997.

Maritain, Jacques. *Art and Scholasticism and the Frontiers of Poetry*. Trans. Joseph W. Evans. New York: Charles Scribner's Sons, 1962.

Pieper, Joseph. *Leisure, the Basis of Culture*. Trans. Gerald Malsbary. South Bend: St. Augustine's Press, 1998.

Taylor, James. *Poetic Knowledge: The Recovering of Education*. Albany: State U of New York Press, 1998.

RE-ENSOULING
EDUCATION

A MORE HUMANE WAY OF KNOWING

The essays in this section all explore two very different kinds of knowing, variously defined as experiential knowledge versus factual knowledge, imaginative knowledge versus empirical knowledge, subjective knowledge versus objective knowledge, mythos-knowledge versus logos-knowledge. Each essay posits the field of depth psychology as a way out of or through this duality because of its radical insight: if we accept the reality of the unconscious, pure objectivity becomes impossible. We become subjective beings who come to know our subjects through our subjectivity. In doing so, we move from stating *what something is* to sharing *what something is like* (Cynthia Anne Hale), from asserting factual truth to exploring psychological truth (Ginette Paris), and from making the quest for the universal and the generalizable our dominant epistemological value to valuing the individual and the particular knower and known (Susan Rowland). This spins our compass away from scientism and propels us toward myth, toward narrative, toward experience, toward perspectivism, and toward imagination.

In other words, we move toward the humanities.

In her essay, Hale is particularly interested in the power of the humanities to "experientially engage us." She writes, "Through the imagination, we hear and see, and even smell, taste, and touch experiences that are not literally our own. Experientially, we transcend an exclusive reliance on rational thought about the perspectives of others. By imaginatively engaging with these realities, we begin to relate to Other." Her essay explores how the arts, humanities, and depth psychology all help us gain greater insight into the experiences of others, *what it is like* to be other than ourselves.

While Hale asserts that depth psychology forms a bridge between the science and the humanities, the next essay by Ginette Paris argues that depth psychology should give up being seen as a science and acknowledge that it more properly belongs to the humanities. While science teaches us to see and value what is factual, depth psychology teaches us to see and value the mythical. "Our personal story is the product of our imagination," Paris writes, and as such, it can be reimagined, or re-mythologized. We must recognize the myth we are living, because it is only through recognizing that we are in a myth that we can change our myth. "Every collectivity is always updating its myths, and if it ever stops doing so, there is stagnation. The same process goes on in the personal psyche: it has to constantly add, cut, paste, save, delete, and sometimes reformat the whole psychic disk, or else it stagnates."

People, whether individuals or collectives, who have lost touch with their living story, with their imagination, with the "irrational and dreaming part of themselves" do more than stagnate, Susan Rowland suggests: they actually become vampiric. "Without imaginative *being*, they are also unconnected to their bodily selves, have no sensing of nature or society and merely prey on others." She lifts the phrase "blood-sucking ghosts" from depth psychologist C. G. Jung, and writes, "Jung's blood-sucking ghosts are the vampires modernity makes when it represses mythos, the natural story spinning threads of the psyche. Logos cannot be healthy with insufficient mythos. Skewed into signifying merely economic well-being, a university is more dead than alive. As mythos, the humanities are about competing visions of self and world. Their debates and inability to agree are aspects of a *living* collective psyche."

All three essays in this section argue that humanity cannot live by logos alone; we need myths, stories, experiences, dreams, images, metaphors, and symbols. Above all, we need the imagination, the eternal flame that has burned for millennia in the humanities.

Jennifer Leigh Selig

The arts, humanities, and depth psychology help us process the world that is around and within us. We return to songs, poems, movies, and paintings because we resonate profoundly with the language of images and symbols. To marginalize their value is to cut ourselves off from a rich path of inquiry and, ultimately, to cut out the emotional layers of what we touch and what touches us.

~Cynthia Anne Hale

Myth contains no certainty, no sure knowledge; it is a product of our imagination. Yet, we cannot live without myths, any more than a culture can survive without literature, art, music, poetry, storytelling, or the form that mythic imagination now takes: cinema, songs, advertisements.

~Ginette Paris

Jung says here that the "living mystery" of the psyche needs more than positivism and empiricism; its needs the imaginative, speculative and critical humanities to be fully human. Concepts with their logical rationality and other scientific modes are important, yet we should not imagine that they can convey the whole truth of who we are.

~Susan Rowland

WHAT IS IT LIKE?
BEING TOUCHED BY THE ARTS AND HUMANITIES IN DEPTH PSYCHOLOGY

Cynthia Anne Hale

A KIND OF INQUIRY

What is it like? I ask this deceptively simple question a lot. Because this kind of open-ended inquiry enables possibility in contrast to fixed answers, I consider it essential to a discussion about the importance of the arts and humanities, particularly as these disciplines relate to depth psychology.

I pose this question to people in all aspects of my life. To a student in a clinical practice class, I may ask it this way: *"What is it like* to feel a client's pain that is in contrast with your own experience?" To a psychotherapy client, I might say: *"What is it like* when your opinion is ignored by your boss?" To a student in a research class, I can say: *"What is it like* for you when you follow your curiosity about your proposed topic?" Many of my friends and colleagues who work as therapists and educators are grounded in depth psychological, archetypal, and mythological approaches, and also value the mutual exploration of *what it is like.*

I also ask myself this question because self-awareness is necessary for processing the perceptions of others. What is my experience, my reality? What is the interplay of my truth when I engage with the perceptions of others? The emphasis of the question, *"What is it like?"* focuses on the assumption that any person can hold a legitimate and yet subjective truth in contrast to an objective, literal, or factual one.

I often am interested in the multi-faceted realities held by others because curiosity is foundational to my work as a depth psychologically-oriented facilitator of change. When researching educational effectiveness or the archetypal nature of the color red, or when teaching the subtleties that connect the art and science of clinical practice, I want to explore what is beyond the surface and beyond myself. When this kind of listening is collaboratively facilitated with self as well as Other, new possibilities emerge. Weaving together different perspectives of *what it is like* enables synthesis as well as deconstruction of the personal with the cultural, of the particular with the universal.

"What is it like?" represents the kind of phenomenological inquiry that is fundamental to the importance of the arts and humanities today, as well as to the creative path they enable for psychologies that extend beyond an individual into their cultural and universal, or archetypal, human experience. Films, paintings, poetry, literature, and music express the realities of our own lives, as well as those of other cultures and times, other people, and even other species. Like art, the symbolic experiences within dreams reflect inner experience, connecting unconscious realms with our ego consciousness. These creative mediums, as well as those of other subjects considered in the broad category of the humanities, such as language, philosophy, and history, experientially engage us. Through the imagination, we hear and see, and even smell, taste, and touch experiences that are not literally our own. Experientially, we transcend an exclusive reliance on rational thought about the perspectives of others. By imaginatively engaging with these realities, we begin to relate to Other.

The foundation established with this kind of inquiry and this kind of relating rests on a simple premise: there is value in reaching beyond the limits of my own perspective. Through image, through metaphor, through the imagination, I myself begin to feel the confusion, triumph, pain, or joy of *what it is like*. And I am touched.

EMOTIONAL ENGAGEMENT

Being touched is a level of emotional engagement that can challenge or validate any assumptions one may have held. A narcissistic comparison of perspectives though—mine vs. yours—retains a rigidity of boundaries that prevents any shift in consciousness. *Being touched* pushes past the borders of what I have previously thought or experienced into more nuance. This action enables me to take it in, or to work with it, as we often say in the world of therapy, creating a kind of exchange that includes empathy and emotional understanding, much more than simply defining distinctions. A co-mingling of divergent perspectives can occur.

In what analytical psychology founder C.G. Jung (1954) described as the transcendent function, going back and forth between opposing views creates great tension. Shifting from one extreme to another requires an enormous amount of psychic energy. Yet by staying with this arduous process, a transcendent perspective may eventually emerge. Not entirely of one previous position or another, yet retaining some essence of each, something new then transcends the old. The kind of creative change occurs that could not have been planned. In this same kind of process, arts, humanities, and depth psychology shift the focus of inquiry from a literal one (*What is it?*) to an emotionally experiential one *(What is it like?)*. New perspectives can transcend those that were previously entrenched.

Depth psychology emphasizes the importance of multi-faceted ways *into* the essence of things. In the psychotherapy of the consulting room, in the scholarship of the classroom, and through the dynamics of the workplace, an archetypal approach in particular considers the experiential, aesthetic, poetic, and mythic aspects of *likeness*. The limitations of intellectual interpretations are challenged. These approaches explore what is beyond the superficial or the obvious and incorporate not only an acknowledgement of the reality of the psyche, but an intentional attunement to the conscious and unconscious forces expressed through images and symbols. "Psyche is a universe, and all study. . . is ultimately psychology," archetypal psychology theorist James Hillman (1975, p. 202) writes in *Re-visioning Psychology*. As expressions of psyche, the arts and humanities provide an experiential path that is built upon a foundation that values reaching beyond the limits of any singular perspective. Through the imagination, we enter other worlds and other perspectives. This immersion into different dimensions of *what it is like* is what moves us.

An immersion into other realms, or into Other, transcends any particular narrative. Agreement or disagreement with any perspective expressed is simply beside the point. A film can give me the experience of walking along a dusty mountain road in a foreign culture. Rhythm and blues or country music take me beyond my conscious thoughts into a universal experience of lost love. By engaging with psyche in these ways, that is, through the imagination in films, in songs, or in books, one can experience multiple realities. Each reality is true for someone, and therefore each is real.

The imagination can be considered a basic reality of human life, and as Roberts Avens' (1980) book succinctly asserts: *Imagination is Reality*. The prejudice he identifies against this reality, as evidenced in western philosophy, makes way for the theory of C. G. Jung, in which the imagination is treated as a psychological necessity somewhat closer to the way it is in eastern traditions. That prejudice continues today and is demonstrated when arts and humanities classes or programs are eliminated as less than essential in education. The imagination is particularly important in the way that its process shapes yet transcends our connections to ourselves and others. Accessing such multiple realities enables what depth psychologist Mary Watkins (2000) calls "dialogue across differences," where processes of non-violent communication and reconciliation can occur. The kind of "dialogue beyond words" (p. 190) she describes depends upon engaging with multiple perspectives as realities, as truths.

SCHOLARSHIP

Entering into these realities through the imagination is important to scholarship as a way of engaging with more than a self-focused and singular lens. If the purpose of scholarship is to facilitate learning that can go beyond current knowledge, to explore and generate the possibility of an unexpected idea, then noticing and privileging multiple realities is particularly important. Through this kind of exploration, a new way of understanding that transcends direct description can begin to develop.

I often begin or end a class with a poem, particularly because what it can evoke is more than I can directly convey. We can consider the images within a poem as expressions of psyche that transcend a literal perspective. In the way that psyche incorporates more than ego and more than intellect, a few words of a poem can grip us on multiple levels. The music that brings me to tears affects me because it has transported me to the very place where I can feel more than the notes, enabling me to experience the emotions of Other as well as my own. I am touched in an imaginative yet embodied way. Inquiry, or research, into these places through the arts and humanities is not only meaningful, but is part of a psychological process that grounds us in our humanity with each other. Precisely because of the splitting and fractures caused by political and religious entrenchment in many cultures worldwide today, more than ever, we need to become fluent with the psychological processes that occur through music, poetry, paintings, and stories. Through these channels, within fictional worlds, differing truths are revealed. Often, they are realities that we may not otherwise encounter or choose to consider.

EXPERIENTIAL INSIGHTS

So far, I have discussed the experiential importance of the arts and humanities and how this kind of experience relates to engaging with the essence of self and Other. In the classroom and in the consulting room, I strive to facilitate a process that enables this kind of experiential engagement to go even further, that is, to create insight.

Many of the students I teach are studying to become psychotherapists.

As they learn the tools of the trade, they begin to engage deeply with the experiences of their clients. Since I have been a therapist for many years, they ask me *what it is like* to engage with the emotional pain of others over time.

One way I answer is by sharing with them a case study from my work as a psychotherapist many years ago with a family of children who were abused by their parents. Although I provide an overview of my understanding of the emotional experience of the children, my focus in the presentation is primarily on how I was affected by working with them, particularly as a new therapist. Through a description of how the course of therapy progressed over four years that is overlaid with my emotional experience, I try to immerse my students in *what it was like*. Most of them readily engage with this process on an empathic level. Knowing that music can facilitate their connection, as well as my own, I begin the class by playing heavy metal music because I want to share the strength I find in its hard rhythms and raw, often angry emotion. I end the presentation with an entirely different kind of music, a Chopin piano concerto that, for me, mirrors the emotional journey I have just shared with them. They may move around, write, or draw during the music. I ask that they concentrate, take it in, and allow this kind of multi-dimensional music to help them process and even digest the confusion of simultaneous emotions such as helplessness and hope.

In this auditory form of preparation and conclusion, we introspectively let ourselves feel into the spaces. Beyond any particular words or images, we feel into the enormity of what is constellated along with thoughts, feelings, and our own personal histories. Group discussion then offers an opportunity to synthesize our emotional reactions with the theoretical aspects of the case. The process exhausts most of us. Somehow, though, this infusion of music into the room, into us really, enables a renewed energy that begins to integrate dark fragments into the light of consciousness.

Of all the classes I have taught through the years, this is the one that students recall to me most often after they have graduated, and I offer its brief description here as an example of how depth psychological learning can be synthesized through the arts and humanities on multiple levels. Although the music in no way literally speaks to their question, it is the most powerful way that I know to punctuate my answer to their question of *what it is like* to be a therapist engaging with realities that defy rational explanation. Each student's particular experience with the music will not necessarily be the same as mine. As we listen together, though, the music both contains and releases the intensity of our emotional connections—to the material, the children, the work, our own histories. It also situates our individual perspectives within universally-experienced energies. In this way, music connects us to the more archetypal magnitude of psychological experience. Our insights can incubate within a context far greater than any of our single perspectives.

SITUATING DEPTH PSYCHOLOGY IN MEDICAL SCIENCE

Since the concern of these collected essays is particularly with the value of the arts and humanities in education itself, I want to turn the question now to more directly address these disciplines and the way that depth psychology represents a field that bridges their inherent values with those of science. For the arts and the humanities, and for the depth psychology that considers them an essential and inevitable expression of psyche, it is important to ask: *what is it like?*

Let's explore how these disciplines have been viewed and how they have related to each other. For at least the past hundred years or so that it has been identified as an academic discipline in the western world, psychology has occupied a strange place somewhere between science and art. From the perspective of the arts, by which I mean any variety of creative expression, psychology appears very scientific. Indeed, many mysteries of the psyche have been shaped to the forms and conventions of western medical science through psyche-logy, or study of the psyche. The early pioneers of depth psychology—Sigmund Freud and C. G. Jung—struggled to articulate these mysteries in the more objective language of psychiatry, or medical science, in order to legitimize their theories of the unconscious psyche. At the turn of the twentieth century, when science was emerging as the most widely accepted way to describe the symptoms and pathologies of life, their allegiance to its approach enabled them to situate psychoanalysis and analytic psychology within medical science. Depth psychology's inclusion of the reality of the unconscious emphasized a relationship to the arts and humanities, however, with its reflections of the mysteries of life through the lenses of emotional experience as in dreams, myth, art, and even, for Jung, in alchemy. Allegiance to both science and art can appear incongruent, particularly for those seeking answers to *"What is it?"* rather than *"What is it like?"* However, a depth psychological incorporation of the arts and humanities provides a multi-dimensional way into things.

The tension of the struggles of depth psychology's founders is one we still hold today. It continues within the western medical science of behavioral health that is promoted and paid for by managed health care insurance. The psychodynamically-oriented approaches of depth psychology still present too much subjectivity for the more mainstream behaviorally-oriented methodologies of psychotherapy. For example, the medical approach reflected in the American Psychiatric Association's (2000) *Diagnostic and Statistical Manual* defines problematic clusters of human behavior. In this particular paradigm, order emerges through a culturally-constructed classification and description of disorders, and the study of the psyche becomes focused and manageable. Although an emphasis on diagnosis alone would be rare for most clinicians today or in the past, depth-oriented psychotherapists tend to work at a distance from this kind of order, preferring to facilitate the connection between inner and outer experience. Prompted by the popular online encyclopedia Wikipedia, I am reminded that medicine is defined as the art *and* science of healing, emphasizing the interconnections.

TEACHING FROM A DEPTH PSYCHOLOGICAL PERSPECTIVE: THE IMPORTANCE OF *WHAT IT IS LIKE*

Practitioners and scholars of depth psychology continue to navigate the mysteries of the human psyche through explorations of symbolic expression in many domains. The creative processes of painting, dancing, performing drama or music, writing poetry or literature, are considered not only legitimate but necessary engagements of human emotional experience with psyche. Faculty members at Pacifica Graduate Institute, where I teach, incorporate these processes into classes or assignments as paths of inquiry and expressions of psyche. Students are encouraged to explore the arts and humanities in their research as interdisciplinary bridges between the physical, concrete aspects of thinking and the symbolic facility of the imagination. Teaching any topic from a depth psychological perspective, then, can incorporate varied perspectives as an on-going creative learning process of interaction between topic, teacher, and students. On intellectual and emotional levels, this kind of creative collaboration inevitably produces shifts of consciousness.

SYNTHESIS WITH DECONSTRUCTION

The arts, humanities, and depth psychology help us process the world that is around and within us. We return to songs, poems, movies, and paintings because we resonate profoundly with the language of images and symbols. To marginalize their value is to cut ourselves off from a rich path of inquiry and, ultimately, to cut out the emotional layers of what we touch and what touches us. Through these disciplines, we utilize emotional engagement to teach students how to host multiple perspectives. Education that incorporates these disciplines creates citizens of the world who can synthesize as well as deconstruct. By asking others *what it is like,* students of the arts, humanities, and depth psychology can relate to any aspect of life more perceptively and with greater insight. They can learn by engaging empathically with other ways of being. As students are touched, this kind of learning radiates out from the immediate moment, and others in the world, too, are touched.

REFERENCES

American Psychiatric Association. 2000. *Diagnostic and Statistical Manual of Mental Disorders.* 4th ed. Washington, DC: American Psychiatric Association.

Avens, Roberts. 1980. *Imagination Is Reality: Western Nirvana in Jung, Hillman, Barfield and Cassirer.* Putnam, CT: Spring Publications.

Hillman, James. 1975. *Re-Visioning Psychology.* New York: HarperPerennial.

Jung, C. G. 1954. "The Transcendent Function." Vol. 8 of *The Collected Works of C. G. Jung.* Princeton, NJ: Princeton UP. 67-91.

"Medicine." Wikipedia entry. Retrieved 29 November 2011.

Watkins, Mary. 2000. *Invisible Guests: The Development of Imaginal Dialogues.* Woodstock, CT: Spring Publications.

BOUNDARY ISSUES:
"YOU, SCIENCE. ME, HUMANITIES."

Ginette Paris

When I was nine years old, one day my father and I were sitting on a bridge stalled in traffic. I saw a man, dressed in a black cashmere overcoat, white silk scarf and a perfect felt hat, leaning over the railing of the sidewalk of the bridge, looking down into the waters of the mighty turbulent river below. I had the sharp intuition, certitude, that he would throw himself from the bridge and said so to my father. Moments later he did; I saw him jump, his hat still on, the white silk scarf unfolding in the air like soft wings. The next day the paper told his story of heartbreak. To the child that I was, this tragedy proved the reality of the soul. There exists something in us, invisible and intangible, that distills suffering and joy. Loss of love, lack of love, failures of love can attack this invisible organ of feeling and we want to jump off a bridge. I had found my vocation and a definition of the soul: that which is invisible, yet experiences all feelings.

At fifty-five years old, after a brain injury and eight months of rehabilitation, I felt the same certitude: the reality of the psyche is invisible yet it qualifies all our experiences; it can turn pain into a gift and a gift into a curse. But knowing something from the heart and finding the language to communicate the experience are two very different things. When the time came for me to get back behind the podium and resume my work as professor of psychology, the panic was intense because I had to relearn how to teach, this time from a place of uncertainty. I had to leave behind the Gnostic stance, to stop posturing as the psychologist who knows about the psyche, and to assume the position of the agnostic, of one who does not know for sure. When I confided this to a friend, himself a professor of literature, he gave me this advice: "I never know for sure the meaning of a poem. Still, I can talk with my students about the poem's evocative power."

That was excellent advice and I followed it. The psyche really is like a poem, it has evocative power and it can be trained to perform with even more power. I finally understood the intellectual liberation that comes with the idea that the entire field of depth psychology can now move back to the original goal, which is to evoke, a verb which means, according to Encarta Encyclopedia: "1. to bring to mind a memory or feeling, especially from the past; 2. to provoke a particular reaction or feeling; 3. to make beings appear who are normally invisible." Symbols are evocative, stories are evocative, art is evocative, literature is evocative, myths are evocative.

The reality of the psyche is a virtual one, based on the psychological imagining or "imaging" we do daily because we need to symbolize events that move us. The goal of an analysis is to become aware of that evocative process, aware of the virtual script we create every minute, aware of the flavor of today's ordinary hypnotic trance, or—to use Joseph Campbell's words—to become aware of the myths we live by. A myth is a powerful suggestion, just like a post-hypnotic suggestion, and it is based on a fiction. A metaphor is a fiction, a symbol is a fiction, just as a sad movie is just a fiction, but it can move us to shed real tears. As Jung described it, a symbol is true inside and false outside. A movie script is true inside (it can move me to tears), yet it is false outside (an invented story). A poem that suggests my heart is a violin playing its sad melody in minor mode is true inside and false outside; a guided relaxation exercise (auto-hypnotic technique) that helps me relax at the dentist by listening to a tape of the sound of the ocean offers only a fictive ocean. All this imagery is made-up, but the evocative power of the images is as powerful as the still incomprehensible magic of love. A myth is never factual in the sense that a detective or a journalist needs a fact to be just a fact. A myth is a fantasy, a preferred lie, a foundational story, a hypnotic trance, an identity game, a virtual reality, one that can be either inspirational or despairing. It is a story in which I cast myself, it is my inner cinema, the motion picture of my inner reality—one that moves all the time. No diagnosis can fix the myth, no cure can settle it, because our inner life is precisely what, in us, will not lie still.

Our personal story is the product of our imagination, a faculty that used to be synonymous with what we now call the unconscious. Imagination is just as good a word as unconscious, which, as Freud himself insisted, is and remains a hypothesis, as unproved and unprovable as the concept of "imagination." It is just a word to point at our tendency to amplify stories and expand them into myth. Myth contains no certainty, no sure knowledge; it is a product of our imagination. Yet, we cannot live without myths, any more than a culture can survive without literature, art, music, poetry, storytelling, or the form that mythic imagination now takes: cinema, songs, advertisements. It is crucial, however, to know that a myth is only a myth; it presents itself as truth, but knowing its fictive aspect gives one the power to edit the story.

Just as one has to be really naïve to confuse an infomercial with information, all the same we don't like those who insist on presenting their organizing myth as the source of causality: "you want me to believe that if you beat your kids today, it's 'because' your dad was an alcoholic? Sorry! I am not buying into your myth!" Such oppressive myths can be deconstructed while useful ones can be amplified. Falling in love is an uplifting myth: "you want me to believe that you are a beautiful, creative, interesting, generous, capable person? Yes, I can relate to you from that script." Certain movies have the power to transform us and it does not matter if we know they are invented stories, because we still feel they are internally true. Their artistic and psychological truth resonates with us; that is why we love the cinema. Nevertheless, as rational beings, we also need a clear distinction between the categories of truth. Factual truth is not the same as artistic or psychological truth, and the difference is crucial. The idea of a reporter who, instead of reporting facts, would weave a plausible fiction, is immensely troubling. A fact should, in principle, never be confused with a fiction, although, as all studies in communication have demonstrated, the confusion is more frequent than we like to admit.

When a myth no longer serves, the first move is usually to label it just that: a myth. We declare something to be "only a myth," when the "lie" in it (the metaphor) no longer works for us. The invented story, the scenario, is then deconstructed. Feminism, anti-racism, ecology, atheism have performed such spectacular "deconstructions." The oppressive myths were revealed as lies: black is not ugly, female is not weak, natural resources are not infinite, religion, churches, priests, and obedience are not essential to spirituality. This process has been called deconstruction, a fascinating demolition derby to scrap oppressive myths. The joy of myth debunking can be intense. The deconstructionists did not invent the concept, just a refreshed theory for it. Deconstruction can also be called the work of intelligence and rationality, as opposed to belief and propaganda. It is a form of lucidity, a seeing through fictions that pretend to be facts.

The first step of myth debunking is usually to produce arguments of reality as evidence of the falsity: "you say that women should not get pilots' licenses because their hormones make them unstable? False! Take a look at the statistics!" We are not yet in myth debunking, just getting the facts right, a first step, because rationality is never enough to get rid of a negative myth.

Only a fresh, lively, charged new myth will carry enough magic to replace the old, negative, tired, abusive, retrograde, finished, exhausted myth. Facts are contradicted by facts, statistics by statistics, data by data, and that is called the scientific approach. But a myth can only be replaced by a myth, a virtual reality by another virtual reality, a symbol by a symbol, a story by a story. Along with the rational arguments aiming at the logical deconstruction, a fresh set of images have to appear, exciting new stories, new interpretations, new episodes in the collective script. The new myth reverses the old values and suggests for example that black is beautiful—or female is beautiful, gay is beautiful, old is beautiful, fat is not abject, atheism is virtuous—and so on with each value that was part of the old oppressive myth.

If one reads nineteenth-century novels, any plot involving a woman who chose divorce had to suggest that the price of such freedom might be more than she could bear. The cultural programming of the time was such that the only virtual game a woman was allowed to play when imagining her life was that of selfless wife, obedient nun, or sexless old maid devoted to Church, aging parents, cats, begonias, and Good Will. Divorce was legal but the literature was undermining the legal gain. Every popular novel involving a divorcee had to show her doomed, a pariah, destitute, a lost soul. By comparison, a slew of movies appeared around 1960 exemplifying a very different script; they depicted women who were not only surviving, but thriving and—oh surprise!—enjoying their freedom. The legal, factual, option of divorce was making its way through literature and movie scripts, some of it written by women as they began expressing themselves as writers and directors and some written by men attuned to the new myth. Every collectivity is always updating its myths, and if it ever stops doing so, there is stagnation. The same process goes on in the personal psyche: it has to constantly add, cut, paste, save, delete, and sometimes reformat the whole psychic disk, or else it stagnates. A destructive myth should be treated like a deadly enemy. The psychic space between the new myth and the old myth often feels like a deadly zone. It is. This is the zone for which depth psychology offers a map, one that shows a completely different topography than the map used for a medical diagnosis.

THE CONFUSING DEFINITION OF DEPTH PSYCHOLOGY

"Depth psychology" is a general term that remains confusing because it defines all approaches that take into account the unconscious dimension of the psyche. Depth psychology was first presented as a victory against the debilitating symptoms of neurosis. Freud's initial positioning was that of a medical doctor looking for causes: if the patient's arm is paralyzed because of a repressed desire to slap somebody in the face, then the psychoanalytic talking cure, in lifting the unconscious repression, would cure the paralysis. It was crucial for Freud and Jung, and the immediate followers of depth psychology, to ally themselves with the medical profession, in order to break the Church's monopoly on the care of the soul. The insistence of the first two generations of depth psychologists on being "doctors of the soul" was a strategic necessity, a useful alliance, a wise posturing. Only the medical model was legitimate enough to allow them to talk about a topic such as sex or a concept such as the unconscious. The title of medical doctor offered the prestige needed to challenge the religious monopoly on moral counseling. But today, many, but not all, depth psychologists (including myself) feel that the need for that strategic alliance with the medical profession has passed. This split is responsible for a real tension, and at times an incompatibility, between approaches which, technically, belong in the category of depth psychology, because they all consider the unconscious dimension of the psyche, but take residence in different academic houses. For example, such psychodynamic theories as those of Kohut, Kernberg, Gunderson, cling to a rhetoric of trauma and treatment, a choice that situates them in direct opposition to many Jungians, post-Jungians and archetypal psychologists such as James Hillman, who is joined by theoreticians from religious studies, philosophy, literary criticism and mythology—all of whom radically place themselves outside of the medical logic.

The deconstructive-reconstructive approach of archetypal psychology examines the reasons for dropping the medical pretense and the benefits of getting rid of the whole lot of useless, unprovable hypotheses by radically separating depth psychology from the field of medicine. It was Freud who began the game of fabricating one hypothesis after another, consistent with the medical persona which was crucial to acceptance within the medical milieu that was his. Yet, at the beginning of his career, Freud had been careful to mention that the unconscious was only a kind of useful hypothesis, still unproven, that the unconscious should never be posited as "real," that it was only a useful concept to start thinking about inner life. Freud also expressed that medical training might be the worst possible preparation for being an analyst. He argued in favor of lay analysis, pointing out that the best training was culture, especially knowledge of literature, philosophy, and anthropology. He admitted that his case histories were more like short stories than medical reports. He explicitly said that his theories were not amenable to experimental confirmation or disconfirmation. It is regrettable that later psychoanalysts weren't able to acknowledge this part of the Freudian legacy; they would have felt more at ease with the fact that depth psychology is mostly literature, but a vitally important and rich form of literature. Freud, after all, got the Goethe Prize for literature, not for medicine.

The production of pseudo-scientific explanations about the psyche—adding to the impressive stack of unproven, unprovable psychological hypotheses—has slowed down in the last decade, mainly because the development of neuropsychology is producing research that is truly amenable to experimental confirmation or disconfirmation. Yet, every year, more of these pseudo-scientific explanations are published, only to be later discarded as junk, as is most of the theorizing about homosexuality, frigidity, hysteria, depression, mood disorders, personality disorders, post-traumatic disorders and most afflictions of the psyche that are not evidently based on a general medical condition.

This intellectual waste is revelatory of a complex of inferiority toward hard science, cluttering the field of depth psychology with the wrong rhetoric. I find it more fruitful to work toward an acceptance of the fact that depth psychology is not a natural science, never was, never will be. It was, is, and shall remain a part of the humanities. The mimesis of science, the language of hypothesis, the obsolete conceptual abstractions, the fake complexity (when the real one is that of the psyche), the battles between schools (hiding a battle of egos); all of it is coming to full stop as depth psychologists begin to speak evocatively instead of dogmatically. Theories that borrow the language of science but without the rigor of the scientific approach are useless as science and useless as literature.

After almost a century of trying to prove psychoanalytic theories right or wrong, depth psychologists have no other choice than to take into account the conclusion reached by their own community of researchers. A former president of the American Psychiatric Association, Alan Stone, professor of law and psychiatry in the Faculty of Law and the Faculty of Medicine at Harvard, in his keynote address to the American Academy of Psychoanalysis in 1996, voiced the consensus: depth psychology belongs to the arts and the humanities, not to science and not to the medical model. He did not specify which of the arts, which of the disciplines of the humanities, but he says this in his conclusion: "psychoanalysis will survive in popular culture as a narrative by which we understand and reflect on the moral adventure of life." In other words, he is saying, without using the word, that psychoanalysis will survive as mythology. A mythology, to take his very words, is precisely "a narrative by which we understand and reflect on the moral adventure of life."

Depth psychologists, as well as their patients, can get back to the task of becoming psychologically wiser, philosophically brilliant, rhetorically inspired, and renew their alliance with the arts. We can, at last, stop trying to cure what will not heal, and fix what will not lie still. We can finally afford to stop the pathetic effort to surpass the Joneses (the scientists). Depth psychology has a niche: the art of creating virtual reality. It does not need to lay its eggs in somebody else's nest. Just as there is no denying the progress of medical research, there is also no denying that the richness of a culture is grounded in the humanities, which nurture the capacity to think deeply about things. Depth psychology, as a theory, is just that: a deep thinking about the life of the psyche and, as such, belongs to the arts and humanities.

SCHOOLS, LABELS, EGOS, COPYRIGHTS, MONEY

Another factor of confusion when defining "depth psychology" comes from the fact that over the past decades, the theoretical boundaries between the many depth psychological schools following Freud, Jung, Adler, Reich, Rank, Lacan, Hillman, Klein, Bion, Winnicott, Bowlby, Kohut . . . have broken down under the influence of the eclectic range of practitioners who are all interested in the unconscious dimension of the psyche, but reject the theoretical strictness of the founding fathers. Training institutes, in opening their doors to social workers, educators, philosophers, have fostered a climate of openness. As these new practitioners are trained in more than one approach, the traditional distinction between the concept of psychotherapy and that of psychoanalysis has also softened. Many practitioners are reluctant to label their approach because they want to avoid cultish overtones of schools based upon one founding father (are you Freudian or Jungian?) or one founding mother (are you Kleinian?).

Following that deconstructive mode, psychotherapy from a depth psychological approach appears under many names: psychoanalytic psychotherapy, psychoanalysis, psychological analysis, analytical psychology. For the sake of simplicity, when in need of exploring differences between schools, (such as that between the strictly Jungian approach as compared to the post-Jungian archetypal approach) I prefer to insist on the theoretical nuances in the thinking, rather than differences in the labeling of the approach.

This vagueness around the label of "depth psychology" echoes the vagueness around the word "psychology". First year students in psychology are invariably confused by the fact that the word "psychology" can be affixed to almost any trend, any problem, any discipline: take the word "neuro" and affix the word "psychology" and you have "neuropsychology" which clearly belongs to science; but then you can also take the word "sport", or "music", or "parenting", or "aging" and affix the word "psychology" and you have four more psychologies: psychology of sport, psychology of music; psychology of parenting, psychology of aging. For some of these "psychologies" it is easy to see how they clearly belong to science: neuropsychology and neuropsychological assessment of memory disorders (such as amnesia, aphasia, apraxia); cognitive neuropsychology and assessment of speech and language disorders; neuropsychological rehabilitation; psychology of learning disabilities (such as dyslexia); psychology of motor development; experimental research in clinical and social psychology; clinical assessment and treatment; developmental psychopathology and gerontology; statistical research in mental health disorders.

It is also quite easy to identify the psychologies that belong in the mixed category of "social sciences": behavioral and cognitive development; social psychology (intergroup behavior, group dynamics, action research, participatory research, attitudes and persuasion, gender identity, sex roles, delinquency, prejudices, styles of leadership, social psychology of organizations, verbal and non-verbal communication, self and social identity); developmental psychology of early attachment (childhood, adolescence, adulthood, lifespan development, transitions, ageing); comparative and intercultural psychology; psychology of moral development; psychology of animal behavior; economic psychology; political psychology, sport psychology.

And last, there are the psychologies that read like essays in the tradition of the humanities, although many of its authors still cling to a rhetoric redolent of social science: environmental psychology; feminist psychology, evolutionary psychology, psychology of religion, psychology of music, transpersonal psychology, ecopsychology, Freudian and post-Freudian psychoanalysis, Jungian and post-Jungian analytical psychology, imaginal psychology, archetypal psychology.

New "psychologies" are added every week, some of them little more than the product of ego-inflated authors trying to sell their copyrighted brand of psychology, others showing real innovation and answering the need to better understand the psyche-soma connection. Publishers' catalogues come up every year with more classifications to organize the genres in which their authors are writing. Students drink it all in and later make their own menu from all those approaches.

This proliferation and specialization can be interpreted as a by-product of the growing psychology industry but it may also signal a turning point in the history of psychology. I believe that the next psychologies will present themselves with clearer identities: on one side the psychologies that belong to science, and on the other side the psychologies that belong to the humanities and are concerned with becoming wiser humans. The richness of any culture is so obviously grounded in scientific progress that we have been inclined to take for granted other kinds of progress. Nevertheless, history is a demonstration of how advances in the humanities are determining of the quality of our existence because they bring a capacity to think deeply about things.

REFERENCES

Stone, Alan. 1997. "Where Will Psychoanalysis Survive?" *Harvard Magazine,* January-February. <http://harvardmagazine.com/1997/01/freud.html>. Accessed 7 January 2012.

This essay is an excerpt from the book *Wisdom of the Psyche: Depth Psychology After Neuroscience* (pages 79-88), published by Routledge in 2007 and reprinted with permission.

ARIADNE'S THREAD AND THE BLOODSUCKING GHOSTS

Susan Rowland

[U]prooted human beings, bloodsucking ghosts, whose emptiness is taken for the
unenviable loneliness of the modern man and casts discredit upon him.
C. G. Jung, *Modern Man in Search of a Soul*

INTRODUCTION

The humanities as taught in universities are under threat. So Professor Stanley Fish informs us from the pages of the New York Times (Fish 2010). In an era of shrinking government support for education, the humanities can neither attract the huge grants of the hard sciences nor substantial fees from students. After all, how can a degree in literature guarantee a lucrative career?

While the threat to the teaching of the humanities in the United States is pervasive and acute, in the UK it is now a matter of announced government policy. Hitherto undergraduate teaching has been almost entirely funded by taxes. This began to change when tuition fees were introduced in the 1990's to contribute a small proportion of the real costs. However, from 2014/15, students will have to pay *entirely* for degrees in the arts, humanities and social sciences. Only STEM subjects (Science, Technology, Engineering and Math) will get any subsidy, limited to 20% of total cost. University education is no longer defined as a public "good."

Such a parlous situation begs a number of questions ranging from the "value" of education to the individual, to its connection to commerce (if any), to the role of the state in providing learning, the nature of a university and, indeed, what we imagine is required by the future. The political and social consequences are profound in reinforcing and even re-erecting class privilege. Now only the wealthy can afford to "risk" studying the humanities. Ultimately, of course, as the name 'humanities' indicates, the current crisis is a challenge to how we define ourselves. This chapter will use some ideas of C.G. Jung to argue that the humanities are essential to the whole enterprise of education whether considered from the perspective of the individual or the nation state. Moreover, the mutable and contested nature of the humanities—all these are core characteristics and strengths to be celebrated. For without this space of interpretative creativity and uncertainty, we are diminished into what Jung called "bloodsucking ghosts" (Jung 1933, 228).

IN PURSUIT OF THE HUMANE HUMANITIES

"The humanities" is an imprecise term. Today it usually signifies a group of academic disciplines that use methods defined as analytical, critical, speculative and in particular, imaginative. Here the humanities are distinguished from subjects using empirical methods of the natural and social sciences. Therefore humanities subjects include classics, history, languages, law, literature, the arts, philosophy and religion.

The history of the humanities and universities is one of combining revolutions and deep continuities. In Ancient Greece, humanities meant the preparation of a citizen. As our politicians like to remind us, this "citizen" was the founder of the first attempt at democracy. "His" education was the organic root of the political system espoused by today's Western states.

Under a less liberal regime in the succeeding Roman Empire, the humanities became the seven liberal arts of grammar, rhetoric, logic, arithmetic, geometry, astronomy and music. Here the emphasis was on the acquisition of skills. The humanities were practices to be developed in a useful life of public duty. Such an attitude of the *practicality* of the humanities extended through medieval education where universities prepared priests and, to a growing extent, young men for government service.

Renaissance Europe saw a shift from humanities as "doing" to a body of knowledge to be studied and augmented. The humanities were now subjects, yet still comparatively restricted when it came to finding them in universities. For until the latter part of the nineteenth century, the universities were devoted to the polishing of gentlemen. By this time, the humanities had acquired a psychological tinge. The humanities were recognized as important for developing a story for national and personal identity.

Here perhaps we see one root of the vulnerability of the humanities today. For surely the arts, history, languages are more popular than ever.

They can be found in the public libraries, the theaters, cinemas and museums that are prized, and often well funded by philanthropic donors. The humanities, so one argument goes, do not need higher education. They will survive, maybe even prosper, outside "disciplinary" constraints.

In one respect this has to be true. Literature, in particular, gets written whether it is absorbed into university "English" departments or not. The Law is one aspect of the humanities that is rarely threatened by cutbacks. Perhaps there is more sophistication in so-called "market forces" than hitherto believed? One way of looking closer here is to complete our story of the changing role of higher education.

For the humanities in universities achieved political potency in the twentieth century. At the end of the nineteenth century began the expansion of degree subjects in the humanities. At last it was possible to study either the literature of one's own language or the history leading to one's own time. This change was not simply the result of the flowering of national imagination. It represented a conservative strategy to cope with the potentially de-stabilizing presence of two new kinds of students: women and lower class men. While on the one hand this was a liberation of human and political potential, this was undercut by the humanities becoming oriented to tell stories of national self-satisfaction.

Such a politicizing of subjects such as literature and history engendered its own reaction. The "culture wars" of the 1960s were deeply of the humanities themselves. For they drew on imaginative, critical, analytical and speculative arguments to portray the existing standard curricular in literature, history, philosophy etc. as dedicated to maintaining existing structures of power. Far from just teaching "the best," the humanities until now were perceived as biased towards retaining the social privileges of certain groups. Why should history be the stories of Great Men? What about a history of poor people, or even women? Why should a literature degree be limited to dead white European males?

Hence behind the diversification of humanities degrees since the 1960s is a complex liberatory struggle. After all, the humanities in the previous century had become about finding a story to define one's place in the world. To the educators of the time, "the world" was a stable place of great nations and "one" was a gentleman of means. By the post 1960s, there was an urgent need for different narratives for a new and challenging set of cultural imperatives. This thread of *narrative* is fundamental to human functioning as I shall argue below.

Of course, this spirit of diversity that created exciting new humanities degrees and revisioned "traditional" ones in turn made the whole enterprise vulnerable in a new political climate. Legislatures had previously acquiesced in supporting curricula devoted to national superiority. Why fund critics of the status quo?

If humanities are the hideous progeny of the critical and speculative mind, they lose friends. If they rely upon imagination, then they lose credibility in a world skewed to value "hard" facts. What is needed is a careful scrutiny of the assumptions about knowledge behind the attack on the humanities. We need to follow Ariadne's thread of *narrative* survival into a labyrinthine world of multiple paths and monstrous "ends."

WHO DO YOU THINK YOU ARE?

Psychology has a fascinating position in ideas about knowledge for it looks both ways. Frequently regarded as a science, especially when allied to medicine, it is studied "scientifically" with experiments and laboratories. On the other hand, depth psychology, which takes the reality of the unconscious psyche as basic to it, is part of a modern revolution in knowledge that subverts "objectivity" itself.

Terms such as "positivism" and "empiricism" are used to describe the lasting scientific principles from the age of Sir Isaac Newton (1643–1727). "Positivism" is a philosophy of science that argues that the scientific method of repeatable experiments is the best approach to both human and physical processes. "Empiricism" argues for the indispensability of observational evidence in knowledge.

Very important in the way such notions became dominant in attitudes to knowledge is the assumption of positivism that what is *repeated*, ahistorical, typical and generalizable is superior in epistemological value to the idiosyncratic. Paradoxically, it may be that one shared factor in what we call "humanities" is the cultivation of the idiosyncratic, the individual, the unrepeatable historical happening, the *particular* experience of that work of art. Certainly positivism and empiricism do not remain unchallenged today from the creative work of science itself.

Contemporary to the spread of the humanities in education is a threefold challenge to the heritage of Enlightenment modes of science. In the first place, both relativity physics of Einstein and quantum theory suggested that how we observe deeply affects what we observe. Secondly, the advent of depth psychology undercut the rational mind as a reliable organ of knowing and thirdly, ideas about language began to destabilize research of all kinds.

One depth psychologist, C.G. Jung was at the forefront of what has been called the postmodern turn. He made fundamental to his psyche-logos the role of the unconscious in refuting claims to absolute or secure knowledge.

Nobody drew the conclusion that if the subject of knowledge, the psyche, were in fact a veiled form of existence not immediately accessible to consciousness, then all our knowledge must be incomplete, and moreover to a degree that we cannot determine. (Jung 1954, para. 358)

What Jung does throughout his work is to follow the thread of this remarkable statement about knowledge and the psyche. He says here that because of what we are, creatures not in full control of our mental states, we cannot know the world absolutely. No system for making knowledge, *no one discipline*, can *solve* the question of knowledge (epistemology) nor fully anticipate the future.

This is Jung's first gift to the humanities: the reality and the potential of the unconscious refuses to bless a limit upon ways of knowing. His second gift is to emphasize that the unconscious is dangerous if ignored. And since the unconscious is home to the non-rational in the psyche, it is the humanities in imaginative and speculative mode that the unconscious craves. We have to break down life and events, which are self-contained processes, into meanings, images, concepts, well knowing that in doing so we are getting further away from the living mystery. As long as we ourselves are caught up in the process of creation, we neither see nor understand; indeed we ought not to understand, for nothing is more injurious to immediate experience than cognition. But for the purposes of cognitive understanding we must detach ourselves from the creative process and look at it from the outside. . . . In this way we meet the demands of science. (Jung 1966, para. 121)

Jung says here that the "living mystery" of the psyche needs more than positivism and empiricism; its needs the imaginative, speculative and critical humanities to be fully *human*. Concepts with their logical rationality and other scientific modes are important, yet we should not imagine that they can convey the whole truth of who we are.

Following on from Jung's approach, Ginette Paris in *Wisdom of the Psyche* makes a wonderful case for depth psychology as humanities, not science and its subject best expressed as the imagination. She goes on to argue for its vital role today in a crisis that has been hidden in plain sight in most western countries: the epidemic of mental distress known as depression, mood or anxiety disorders. I want to connect this stunning argument with a defense of the humanities in the common thread of narratives.

ARIADNE AND VAMPIRES

Jung's work offers a third and deeply satisfying support to the humanities in his development of the term "personal myth" and its opposition to the vampire (Jung 1961/1989, 199). In fact, arguably, Jung warns us that we create vampires if we omit the narrative and imaginative arts of the humanities. Without actually using the word "vampire", he describes in an essay published in English in 1933, those who have no psychic connection to the past as "blood sucking ghosts." It is not just that these vampiric creatures have failed to read a history book, rather they have no sense of self, no roots beyond the immediate present.

Jung's vampires have no connection to the irrational and dreaming part of themselves. Without imaginative *being*, they are also unconnected to their bodily selves, have no sensing of nature or society and merely prey on others. They lack an "inner thread" to the darkness in themselves that would enable them to strike a light. Such a thread would also find itself connected to other people and social institutions. Indeed, what I am describing in Jung's bloodsucking ghosts sounds like the profile of a terrorist today. It is a facile but not irrelevant comment that suicide bombers recruited from the universities tend not to be studying humanities.

For the thread to link self and society is explored by Jung in the term "personal myth". This is a story for a life that is a living psychic entity. It is generated by dialogue with the collective unconscious that will supply archetypal imaginative energy to the images thrown up by a particular society. Personal myth is personal and unfixable because it must alter to continually *embody and be enacted by* a particular life. Like the humanities themselves, personal myth is dedicated to the individual and particular. Also like the humanities, personal myth is about creatively dealing with the tension between the particular and wider society.

However one defines the humanities, either as the practices of a true citizen or as subjects to be studied, they are devoted to making a *personal* myth within *collective* meanings. Jung's vampire is one who cannot do this. Humanities in universities facilitate the making of a personal myth by developing critical, speculative and imaginative faculties, by exploring the *contested* narratives of self and nation, and by encouraging students to debate and re-imagine their stories of being in the world.

Vampires, of course, are alienated beings. In restricting a university to positivism and empiricism, are we creating an education in a fantasy of soul-lessness that is so divorced from nature that it believes it cannot die? Such an education proves impotent in a real crisis such as melting polar ice. Although science using positivism and empiricism does invaluable work, why doesn't their huge quantity of empirical evidence persuade the nations that man-made climate change must be addressed? What is wrong with our attitudes to this science that we both privilege and ignore it?

One who was also privileged and ignored was Ariadne who has a claim to be the "mother" of the thread that "makes up" our being. Daughter to King Minos of Crete, Ariadne was part of a structure where the monstrous was out of control. Her half-brother was the Minotaur, part bull, part human, offspring of an illicit union between his mother and Zeus as a bull. Hidden in a labyrinth beneath the Palace, the Minotaur was appeased by human sacrifices from Greece sent as yearly tribute. One year Theseus, the son of the King of Greece, concealed himself amongst the prospective sacrifices. He aimed to end this brutal practice but he could not do so alone.

Understood symbolically, there are several interpretations of this situation. Perhaps the myth reaches back to a past of real human sacrifices to the gods. Archaeological evidence suggests that the bull was sacred in Crete and that a ritual sport of leaping over the horns of the animal was integral to the society. Certainly the story of divine, animal and human sexual congress implies anxiety over pollution of the category "human". Also significant is that Theseus alone is unable to end a custom of crude sacrifice of libido (human tribute) to the part-animal aspect of the collective psyche. What is needed is more than a male hero.

In fact, Theseus has to embrace the anima or feminine for this psychic situation to evolve productively. Ariadne gives Theseus a thread by which he can find a path through the labyrinth in order to kill the Minotaur. Her thread also enables Theseus to escape its deathly shades. Perhaps the thread is a thread of narrative as an enduring connection to the feminine by which Theseus manages to extinguish the reality of brutishness within the polis. If so, then it is unfortunate that Theseus in turn betrays Ariadne. He abandons her on the island of Naxos. There she experiences despair before attracting the attentions of Dionysus. Divine union with him is far from the carnal animality of her mother's fate. Rather, she is risen to the stars.

Theseus does not escape the feminine by literally turning his back on her. The myths record that he does not achieve a lasting relationship. Late in his life, his son, Hippolytus, by the woman he best loved who died in battle, himself is tragically desired by his stepmother, no other than Ariadne's sister. One dimension of the gender struggles here may be the transition between earth-centered goddesses and the arrival of a patriarchal sky-father pantheon. Here the scant archeological evidence implies the very earliest religion to be of a feminine sacred earth. Here the divine is immanent in matter, the most likely religious expression an animism in which tree, rock, water and *place* are all inspirited and can speak to human beings.

In the Neolithic farming period, sky father gods arose to proclaim a creator god who is transcendent of his material creation. Here is a model of creation as *separate* from creator. The struggles between these fundamental structuring powers are played out in the Greek myths and pantheon. Traces of early divine elements remain in Ariadne's *thread*, as aspect of a goddess where human consciousness figures as a web of connections between self and other, ego and unconscious, human and animal and divine.

Descended from Ariadne's thread is narrative itself, the activity of story-making (defined as fictional or truthful) that *connects* across psyches, time-periods and across categories like human and natural. If (like Theseus) we hang onto Ariadne's thread as storytelling, then it becomes a means of going into the dark to deal with monsters. Here we have a basic division of myth familiar to Plato and Aristotle: between *mythos* and *logos*.

Mythos means that *story* is a form of knowledge in itself. It is its own foundation: narrative is a way of knowing that differs on each telling without possessing a perfect or ideal form. In contrast, logos is the abstract knowledge that myth points to. It might be the kind of abstract knowledge that modern science seeks. Or logos could be allegorical such as in Christianity, what appears to be mythos, the primacy of the Christ story, is more properly logos in that all Christ-like stories refer back in meaning to the *one story* that is abstracted and considered as transcendent above the material world.

Put another way, logos figures dualism, a perfect ideal world of form versus an actual living world of faulty particularity. Mythos is recurrent stories but no one instance is more "true": it figures no other. Hence mythos is the guardian of the humanities with its respect for the unique within the recurrents of human living. Mythos, "personal myth", storytelling—these are the threads that embody the humanities.

The distinction crucial to the contemporary threat to the humanities is not between true or fictional narrative. It is not between arts/humanities and sciences/math. For science and math are taught and transmitted as part of stories we tell about ourselves in the world. The distinction is fundamentally between *mythos knowing* of the contingent and particular and *logos knowing* of the ahistorical and transcendent. The arts and humanities are the arts of narrative, whether it becomes the history of the helmet or of Odysseus in modern guise or in social sciences, how the Romany educate their children.

Narrative is used by the favored STEM disciplines but rarely studied by them. Science, technology, engineering and mathematics will suffer without

Ariadne's thread to guide then in and out of the labyrinths of modern perils like climate change. The humanities are the powerhouse of personal myths for their societies. Remove them and those generations are left in the dark without a thread. In the dark, our imaginary monsters become alive. Left too long in the dark and those shorn of the story-making capacity may regress. They suck blood.

Jung's blood-sucking ghosts are the vampires modernity makes when it represses mythos, the natural story spinning threads of the psyche. Logos cannot be healthy with insufficient mythos. Skewed into signifying merely economic well-being, a university is more dead than alive. As mythos, the humanities are about competing visions of self and world. Their debates and inability to agree are aspects of a *living* collective psyche.

It is time for Ariadne to thread her way home.

REFERENCES

Fish, Stanley. 2010. "The Crisis of the Humanities Officially Arrives." *New York Times,* 11 October.

Jung, C. G. 1933. *Modern Man in Search of a Soul.* Trans. W. S. Dell and C. F. Baynes. Orlando, FL: Harcourt, 1933.

———. 1954. *On the Nature of the Psyche.* New York: Routledge, 1954.

———. 1966. *Spirit in Man, Art, and Literature.* Vol. 15 of *The Collected Works of C. G. Jung.* Ed. and trans. Gerhard Adler and R. F. C. Hull. Princeton, N.J.: Princeton UP.

———. 1961/1989. *Memories, Dreams, Reflections.* Recorded and edited by Anna Jaffé; trans. R. Winston and C. Winston. New York: Vintage, 1989.

Paris, Ginette. 2007. *Wisdom of the Psyche.* New York: Routledge, 2007.

THE GREAT STORIES OF HUMAN LIFE

Each of the essays in this section explores what Robert Romanyshyn calls "the great stories of human life." The writers all convey, with a certain tone of nostalgia, a love affair with language, starting with Romanyshyn and the Sunday evening dinner rituals of his youth, when his mother extinguished his father's cigarette as his father prepared to tell a story. Romanyshyn reflects, "In those moments I was living within a symbolic world of images created in ritual space and time, a world of tales woven through the magical play of words. Another vision was born on those Sundays, another way of seeing, and another way of being in and knowing the world. The path that was first opened through the smell of books now was sign-posted: learn the great stories of human life to be found in literature, mythology, film, poetry, drama and history itself as a collective story."

It is these collective stories that Paul Zolbrod wants to share with his students in his post-retirement years teaching early American literature at a small college in the Southwest, but his students have embraced technology at the expense of the written word. Zolbrod waxes eloquent about growing up in the depression, sharing his schoolboy recollections about his initiation into classic literature. "Nostalgic for such a time," he writes, "I still wish to impart the best of those ideals to the students I now teach, which I believe is essential if we are to save our democracy and preserve our humanity."

Kathryn LaFevers Evans' essay takes up the power of language. "The humanities, through the language of epic poetry and other mythologies, open our minds to that timeless great heart of humanity, so that we can invent—can co-create—the best possible future for humankind." Using the recent example of Egypt gaining its freedom to pursue democracy, she writes, "Along with freedom from exterior oppressions, it's also inner freedom that our soul is crying out for, isn't it? Each of us wants to find out for ourselves what really makes us tick, what our individual authentic Self, the heart of our soul, truly is. We want the freedom to think for ourselves, and discovering what that truly means is an inborn right." This leads her to conclude, "A true university offers, within fully developed programs and majors, the full range of human endeavors."

Dennis Patrick Slattery's essay speaks to the way that the multiple disciplines within the humanities can together amplify this "full range of human endeavors." Slattery came to his passion for the humanities through the portal of literature first, opening his essay with a delightful story of how he would feign illness as a child to stay home, and under the covers of the fort he built in his bed, read a stack of books while listening to his little cream-covered plastic radio. This love of language and story eventually expanded into "an eclectic learning style firmly riveted in the humanities." Through climbing out onto the various branches that make up the tree of the humanities, Slattery learns "that there existed something essential about the way these disciplines related to one another and could be studied within an imaginal container of mirrors, each refracting off one another to reveal what the others did not." He continues, "The humanities behave as a constellation of consciousness-altering disciplines; when taken together, they can evoke and provoke one into a fuller awareness, to see below the phenomenal world into those principles and patterns that give them their structure and form." His conclusion summarizes the conclusion all the essays in this section suggest: "Absent the humanities, this slumber will continue in the modern mind to darken the possibility of an informed and thoughtful collective that has been evaporating on the horizon of culture for decades."

Jennifer Leigh Selig

Lingering at the abyss, I have come to realize two things. One is that the path into the mess of mind is only through soul as the depth of mind. The second is that on this path one needs more than a technical education. One needs an education in the liberal arts and the humanities, because its stories, images, characters situate one's life in the context of the human condition. In that greater frame we come to understand that within the pieces of one's life there is another pattern of which we are not the makers.

~Robert Romanyshyn

Likewise, print's capacity for speaking silently calls for an exclusively internalized focus, leaving the mind itself to build its own imagined reality independent of all the senses. It liberates the individual from the constraints of space and time through a process of self-reliance that leads to an altered awareness of the immediate present. . . . I wish, therefore, that students could learn better to travel inward, where in Walt Whitman's terms, they can loaf and invite their souls.

~Paul Zolbrod

There is no deeper soul from which to be perpetually reborn, re-invented, than the hidden chamber of the human heart. The humanities are an essential conduit for the expression of heart out into the greater world. . . . The shared heart that's taught from generation to generation through the humanities is where we will find our true sense of One-ness, of peace.

~Kathryn LaFevers Evans

These early experiences forged in me an interest in learning, never mind through what archway or series of metaphors; the shared values, however, were in reading, writing and speaking. The mystery and power of language itself to convey realities independent of and beyond the scope of my narrow world of experiences, to enliven and quicken my imagination to envision and at least grasp tentatively the problems inherent in different clusters of study, filled my existence with insights into the hidden and invisible realities of the world I could experience through the senses.

~Dennis Patrick Slattery

LINGERING AT THE ABYSS

Robert Romanyshyn

—-easy is the descent to Avernus:
night and day the door of gloomy Dis stands open:
but to recall one's steps and pass out to the upper air,
this is the task, this is the toil.
~Virgil

THE GARDEN

A ritual opens almost all my days now, a practice that stitches together
the worlds of night and day. Over strong, hot coffee and jellied, buttered
toast, my wife, Veronica Goodchild, and I sit in the garden. Here the spiral
of every new day begins and in this place we tell our dreams, those treasures
of the night, which with their mysteries and shadows seek some light. But
as we talk we are also drawn into that other light, the *lumen naturae*, the light
of nature whose wisdom is older that our light, the light of mind. As we talk
the birds sing and on occasion Frazier, the cat that we adopted—or was it
he who adopted us?—strolls into the garden, stops by us to say his hello,
then regally sits at the border between deck and lawn to survey his domain.
Dream talk and bird song and cat-like grace weave together in these
moments as the day begins. And on occasion, when the coffee and toast are
finished, and the birds have taken wing and Frazier has begun his daily
rounds, I linger for a time and wait as the garden becomes a place of reverie.
Reverie, I have come to appreciate, is the capacity to be useless and as such
it is the seedbed of imagination.

This essay, which tells the tale of bridge-building between the worlds
of night and day, of dream and imagination, and of a bridge whose materials
are and have been the liberal arts and the humanities, and of a building that
continues, began in a garden reverie. It is an essay, which like the humanities

and liberal arts themselves, is useless and because of that, necessary.

THE LIBRARY: PART ONE

More than a half century ago I had an experience that in retrospect has proven itself to be a pivotal moment in my life. One of my sisters, who was six years older than I, invited me one summer morning to walk with her to a place called a library. I was at the time maybe 9 or 10 years old and my summer days were precious moments to be spent with my pals, roaming like a small tribe through various neighborhoods, causing as much mischief as we could, straying as close as possible to the line dividing mischief and that something other, which at that age felt exciting and forbidden. Girls were yet on the horizon, although a few of us now and then caught glimpses of them and wondered about their mystery. Having two sisters, the other one being just a bit younger, had taught me that girls were maybe more trouble than they were worth, a sentiment that shortly gave way to another opinion. Be that as it may, after some hectoring by my sister I agreed that morning to accompany her, and we began our walk, which, while in measured space, was no more than a few blocks, opened a path into a new world.

I still remember the light that streamed through the windows. It had a soft, buttery color to it as it was filtered through shades that had a light brown tone. Yellow, and particularly a yellow with that quality to it, is still my favorite color, which has convinced me over the years that our desires are awakened in relation to our encounters with the world. In addition, that moment of crossing the threshold into the library also held something else, a quality that resonated so deeply in my bones that when I exited the library—how long was I there?—I was someone else.

It was the smell of the books—musty, old, leathery, thick and enveloping! I was struck dumb. The threshold marked a transition. On one side was the young vagabond, content to roam the streets of life with his tribe, unburdened and free. On the other side—well that is the tale of this essay!

THE LIBRARY: PART TWO

To this day I wonder what the arc of my life would have been if the library on that day had been filled with computer terminals. I shudder to think of it, although in some strange, elliptical way the book that I wrote on technology—*Technology as Symptom and Dream,* seems a dead giveaway now, and almost pre-ordained—might have had its roots in that fertile soil where the event and its memory intertwine in that subtle space where re-membering is a creative act, where, as the poet John Keats has told us, the world is the vale of soul making, that place where the alchemy of life takes place, leavening the facts of life with the spices of the imagination.

That musty dark and rich odor of the books haunted me. I had to go back. I had to discover the many treasures buried in those tomes. Gradually over the next few years I spent less and less time with my tribe. I was suspended between a visible world made of things and the invisible worlds made of words. Getting my library card was my first graduation; my first passport into that other world

I soon learned the ways of that place, especially how to sneak into the section reserved for adults. The plethora of books and the titles on their spines promised exciting but vague adventures. One day one book in particular caught my eye—*Three Essays on a Theory of Sexuality*—by someone whose name seemed quite foreign, maybe even un-American. Remember, it was the time of the McCarthy witch-hunts, where everyone was looking for a communist under the bed. But communists under the bed did not at all interest me. What did intrigue me, however, was the possibility of secreting that book under my bed. That thought and the horizon where those alien creatures called girls lingered banged into each other, a big bang of the mind, that gave me a headache. I had to have that book. But getting it was impossible. I was not yet 12 years of age.

Luck, or perhaps I should say destiny, intervened. Near the shelf where that forbidden fruit lay was a window whose bottom half was left open on warm summer days. Sure that no one was watching I took that book, walked to the open window and tossed it outside. Casually strolling past the library matron—and no other word will do here for a twelve-year old boy—I smiled and exited the library. When I got home I hid the book under my bed and waited for the night. In the dim light of a flashlight I opened it and was disappointed. Not only did it not have any pictures, it made no sense of that mystery of sex. I could not understand a word.

I never returned the book. My library fine must now be in the thousands of dollars. It would be worth every penny, however, because my life in academia began with that theft. Moreover that life had its own particular shape. My life in academia began under the covers and in the dim light of night. I became a psychologist, but a psychologist of a certain type. And herein the tale continues.

THRESHOLDS, BORDERS AND BRIDGES

Between that transgression—and it is ever so sweet and so necessary a part of life to cross borders, an act which on an archetypal level is guided by Hermes, the guardian of boundaries and the protector of travelers who cross them, the thief, the messenger between worlds, the guide to the underworld, the trickster, and the one for whom hermeneutics is named, a not so incidental fact in my development—and this next moment, much water had passed under the bridge. I was hungry, an eater of words, awash in the fantasies unleashed by books and music. This other world was as real as the bricks and stones world and somehow they belonged together, the fantasies weaving themselves around things, like a spider's web, so delicate and fragile and strong. Novels, plays, poems, history and philosophy too were my diet, while Beethoven's symphonies with their thundering tempos set a rhythm to my days and Rimsky-Korsakov's *Scheherazade* filled my dreams with beautiful, sultry women and fantasies of high dramas and daring heroics. And there was Mahler's music too—brooding dark, melancholic—that hinted at depths and dark places.

My father saw something of this change. While he hoped I would attend the high school where I would receive a technical and scientific education—he was a master builder, a genius with wood and all materials, a craftsman of the highest order—he supported my choice to attend a high school whose curriculum was devoted to the liberal arts. And it was there that an event occurred, which was as transformative as the theft. I was introduced to the wonder of language, to the living reality of words. I was introduced to Latin!

In looking back I have realized that my father supported my choice because he was also a maker of another kind, a crafter of stories. The Sunday dinner table around which he, my mother, two sisters and I would gather was a bridge built of tales told within a ritual space. It was the bridge between those two moments in the library and the first declension of Latin nouns with their mysteriously beautiful case endings whose chant still lingers in a subtle way, like the scent of a sweet flower hovers around you after you have passed by (*femina, feminae, feminae, feminam, femina/feminae, feminarum, feminis, feminas, feminas*) and the equally mystifying genders (how extraordinary it was to learn that the word road—*via*—was feminine—a jewel that has to make one stop and think about the roads less traveled). Oh, those clever Romans! So transformative were these moments that when recently I returned to my high school for a 50th reunion I refused to give a donation because I learned that they no longer taught Latin.

AT THE DINNER TABLE

There was a pattern to these Sunday dinners, a ritual that my mother and father practiced with a certain religious zeal. After the meal was finished, and it was always a special Sunday dinner that was eaten slowly and with a kind of sacred quality that made the meal into a communion, my mother and father would commence the ritual.

My father would light a cigarette and my mother would sip her tea. After a few puffs my after-dinner-father, in his white undershirt and wreathed in smoke, which always looked to me like a cloudy crown or halo around his head, would sit back, take a deep breath and prepare to tell his story. Before he could begin, however, my mother would carefully put down her cup of tea and say, "Pete, give me a puff of your cigarette." My father would always reply, "Eleanor, this is my last one. Don't drop it in your tea." Of course, that is exactly what would happen. She would take the cigarette, take her one puff and, preparing to hand it back, she would drop it in the tea.

Sunday after Sunday the same drama was enacted, and each time it was as if a curtain was being raised for a play to begin. And indeed that is what it was—they were playing with each other. It was, as I later came to suspect, their way of loving each other, as counter-intuitive as that might seem. No one ever got angry, and indeed the ritual was the prologue to the stories.

On that stage, in the context of that ritual, the quotidian world of Sunday dinner was magically transformed. No camera could ever record such a magical change because the change was not a matter of fact. Nor was it an idea in my mind. It was of another kind of reality. In those moments I was living within a symbolic world of images created in ritual space and time, a world of tales woven through the magical play of words. Another vision was born on those Sundays, another way of seeing, and another way of being in and knowing the world. The path that was first opened through the smell of books now was sign-posted: learn the great stories of human life to be found in literature, mythology, film, poetry, drama and history itself as a collective story.

The bridge that was built on those Sundays led to the therapy room, that space where speech occurs, that place where for more than thirty years I, as a depth psychologist, listened to stories, and as a patient crafted my own. But on the way, I had to learn another lesson. The bridge that is woven of stories is also made of dreams. And therein begins another chapter of this story.

KEEPING SOUL IN MIND

The amphitheater was enormous. At least 150 students were in the introduction to chemistry class, which was the first required step in the pre-med program. All those great stories were creations of the human mind, and in my second year of college I was taking the class that would lead to medical school and a specialization in psychiatry. I lasted about one week before a dream changed my course.

In the dream I am walking down a long hallway in an office building. Ahead of me at the far end of the corridor I see light shining through a frosted glass door, the kind of glass that one might see on the door to a doctor's office. I knew in the dream that my name would be stenciled on that glass. As I drew nearer to the door I could see the writing. Indeed, my name and title were clearly visible: Robert D. Romanyshyn, M.D. Surprisingly, however, below my name was the area of my medical specialization. The word in bold black-stenciled letters was Proctologist. Sometimes, as I would learn over the course of the next fifty years of working with dreams, dreams can be a "pain-in-the-ass"!

Untutored, naïve at that time in my life about ways of working with the dream, I did know that there were people who took them as sources of meaning and value. Subsequent to my disappointment with my earlier nighttime undercover work with Freud, I had taken up many of his works, especially *The Interpretation of Dreams*, and from that reading I knew that this dream was engaging me. In my primitive way, in a kind of early practice of the art of interpretation, I took the symbols to mean that the path of medicine would be a downward move from the clarity of mind to the messy ambiguity of 'shit'. That interpretation turned out to be one of those fateful detours that brought me in a very circuitous way to the place where I am today, where—A*mor fati*—I am where I am supposed to be.

In retrospect—we are always playing catch up with the dream—the dream in its deeper wisdom made a mess of my plans. The day following the dream, I dropped the chemistry course and enrolled in an introduction to psychology class. On that path, which for some twenty-five years took me deeper into philosophy and the cultural and historical aspects of western culture, I would discover that the 'Gold' of all our splendid achievements would be found, as the alchemist of old had said it, in the 'shit'. But the path could not be through psychiatric medicine. To appreciate that wisdom I had to be educated. I suspected that psychology would foster that education.

Initially, however, I thought I had made a mistake because the text for the class was a classic one at the time, which opened with the claim that psychology is a science and proceeded to demonstrate that claim with chapters that explained psychological experiences in terms of their biological foundations. Something seemed not quite right in all this. Was psychology just 'bad medicine' which would not help me find the alchemical gold in the symbolic shit? To be told, for example, that the perception of a beautiful sunrise was the addition/projection of a meaning—beauty—onto the convergence of physical sensations and physiological processes was

44

disappointing. The explanation not only took me away from the experience, it also posited a split between an inner psychological world of meaning and value and an outer world of material forces. My disappointment felt like a repeat of my earlier undercover nighttime work in psychology. But there was a difference. Earlier I had not understood a word of Freud's essays on sexuality. Now I understood the words that placed a gap between my perceptual experience and its explanation, and I did not like what I was hearing. In that gap between the discourse of psychology and the direct encounter of the world in its immediacy I felt lost, like a homeless orphan. Where was my discipline? Should I leave that class as well and go into literature?

Detours require faith. Paths that deviate from a road that one has mapped out in advance require that one surrender to some deeper impulse, like the wisdom of a dream. Sometimes such faith is rewarded; sometimes one just stays lost. In this instance my faith, a kind of dumb animal stubbornness, paid dividends, because in the final two classes the professor—Amedeo Giorgi—addressed this problem indirectly when he introduced us to phenomenology. Two lectures by a professor who was an experimental psychologist and who was radically changed by his encounter with phenomenology, which at that point—1962—was a new wave in psychology making its way across the ocean from its European home to America's shores. Two lectures and I was hooked. Turning down lucrative fellowships to four prestigious programs in clinical psychology, I accepted an assistantship and followed Giorgi to Duquesne University, where the first program in phenomenological psychology was starting.

Of all the things that one can say of phenomenology, the one that is the simplest and, I think, the most revealing, is encoded in the word itself. Phenomenology is the logos of phenomena, the speaking of the things of the world as they show themselves. Back to the things themselves, Husserl, the father of modern phenomenology, had said, and in that return to the world the phenomenologist was the one who would lend an ear and in so doing become a spokesperson for the world.

With Maurice Merleau-Ponty, Martin Heidegger, Jean-Paul Sartre and others as companions, my psychology was being deeply rooted in philosophy, and with Gaston Bachelard, J.H. van den Berg and again Sartre among others, my ear was becoming attuned to the poetic resonances in phenomenology. In addition, I began to see how phenomenology was a foundation for a psychology whose mind was flesh. Indeed, for Merleau-Ponty phenomenology was a love affair with the world, an erotic bond between the flesh of body and that of the world, a way of knowing the world and being in it in which language was embedded in the sweet seductions of desire between the sensual embodied mind and the sensuous world.

In the stream of life it is the invisible undercurrents that move us along. Swept away from medicine and a career in psychiatry, I was carried into phenomenological psychology, which became for me a bridge with the philosopher on one side and the poet on the other. On the bridge I wrote my early books and articles in the 1970s and 80s, most of which leaned toward the side of philosophical and historical studies of cultural phenomena. But the dream was not finished with me. There was still some 'shit' to deal with and on the horizon Freud was making his return, peeking his head out as it were, from under the covers. Merleau-Ponty in his final works had in fact turned phenomenology toward a dialogue with psychoanalysis and I had become part of that conversation in some of my publications. Shortly, as we say, the shit would hit the fan, and when it did the bridge collapsed into the yawning abyss that lay beneath it. On the way down, in free fall, I was given life-lines. One was from Jung and the other from the poets. Before the fall, however, there was one moment that foreshadowed it. In a library in Trinity College while on a trip to Dublin I saw in a manuscript these three words: "*Sapientia est excrementum.*" Knowledge is shit, expressed in a language that I had learned to love so long ago.

LINGERING AT THE ABYSS

At the Sunday dinner table my love for the magic and power of language was first born, and in the exposure to Latin a deep appreciation for the family kinships among words was seeded. To be writing an essay, for example, on desire and to hear in that word its Latin root—*desiderare*—draws one into the depths of desire in relation to the stars, unfolding an image of how we, suspended between earth and the heavens, are drawn out of ourselves in longing toward the horizon, that place that nowhere is always now-here as a subtle promise that earth and sky do meet, that our longings do matter. Literature, history, art, philosophy and poetry e-*ducated* me into those longings. These liberal arts have informed my life as therapist, teacher and writer.

The figures of literature personified my imagination and gave it character. Their stories taught me that life as lived is about creatively *re-membering* the plot lines of one's life, an on-going work of the imagination. The DSM manual, which is the bible of clinical diagnosis, has always struck me as plot lines in search of their characters. The figures of soul who crowded my consulting room came in the guise of literary characters.

Indeed, through literature I learned to appreciate the therapy room as that place where the persons who come to therapy are transformed into the figures of soul who come to tell their tales.

In my passion for history I learned that the past lingers in the present and that the way in which we re-member the past shapes the ways in which we imagine a future and vice versa. The past that lingers as symptom and opportunity waits for us with its unfinished business by the side of the road, and in attending to its summons we take up a heritage as a destiny. My first two books—*Psychological Life From Science to Metaphor* and *Technology as Symptom and Dream*—were made in that work of *re-collecting* soul left by the side of the road in psychology.

Art schooled me in the love of images and taught me the miracle of wonder and the delightful pleasures of reverie, which in their being useless are the most useful. Essays like "Angels and Other Anomalies of the Imaginal Life" and "Psychology is Useless; Or it Should Be" collected in *Ways of the Heart* are testimony to the fact that the ability to stay in the place between matters of fact and ideas of mind is and has been a matter of heart.

As much as the above disciplines have had an informative and enduring influence in my life and work as a psychologist, therapist, writer and teacher, philosophy and poetry stand out as boundary markers bridging that place of the between. Indeed, over the years I have come to realize that philosopher and poet have been the constant companions in and vivid personifications of my interior life. What I think and write and how I think what I think and write what I write is always mediated between them. To riff on the title of the essay in this volume by my good friend Michael Sipiora, psychology for me is and has been unthinkable without them. Between the philosopher on one side and the poet on the other I have learned to value the beauty and clarity of ideas and the rhythms, melodies and tempos of language.

Reading some of the major philosophers who have shaped the western mind form antiquity to postmodernism, I came to value not just the thoughts that were thought, but also and perhaps more deeply the alchemy of thinking, whose magic invites me to hold onto ideas by letting go of them. And in the company of the poets, I was tutored in the arts of attending to the mystery of the moment and schooled in that devotion to words that somehow are so responsive to what in those iconic epiphanies when the simple reveals itself as uncanny, when the ordinary becomes extraordinary, is present in its absence. Indeed, reading poetry is a daily ritual for me, a meditative practice that slows the rush of time and thereby cultivates the slower, dreamy rhythms of soul. And in this ambience of poetry Orpheus, the eponymous poet, is always near. The only poet whom Plato allowed back into the Polis, Orpheus, who is the poet of love, loss, descent and transformation, is the figure who sculpts my flesh into that gesture of soul making, that backward glance through which the primary work of soul, the work against forgetting, is done, that companion whose underworld eyes reveals the miracle in the mundane.

But who has time for such things, for these slower rhythms of soul making? What good is an education in the humanities, especially in an age ruled by what Heidegger calls calculative thinking and in which professional psychology seeks to define itself apart from the humanities in terms of the acronym STEM—education in terms of Science, Technology, Engineering and Mathematics?

In 1991 I was faced with this urgent and serious question addressed to the core of my life when my wife of 25 years died suddenly and without warning. In that moment, everything that I was and had been and imagined being, and everything that I knew fell into the abyss. In the turbulent waters of that underworld grief only one thing kept me from drowning. By my bedside I kept and read each night some passages from *The Tempest*. Each night Prospero would enter my room and in the image of shipwreck my own shipwreck slowly, very slowly, found a larger tale. My wrecked soul was also buoyed by his words: "We are such stuff/ As dreams are made on, and our little life/ Is rounded with a sleep."

Sapientia est excrementum! Knowledge that does not stir the depths before it reaches the surface of mind, that does not wound in its teaching is shit. But knowledge that is gained in the depths, in the pathos of the wound, is also shit, the kind that hides the alchemical Gold.

Lingering at the abyss I have come to realize two things. One is that the path into the mess of mind is only through soul as the depth of mind. The second is that on this path one needs more than a technical education. One needs an education in the liberal arts and the humanities, because its stories, images, characters situate one's life in the context of the human condition. In that greater frame we come to understand that within the pieces of one's life there is another pattern of which we are not the makers.

In the foreword to *The Soul in Grief*, which I wrote seven years after the death of my wife, Thomas Moore described it as ". . . a form of education of the deepest sort." That book and those that have followed, especially *The Wounded Researcher*, which makes a case for the necessity to include the depths in our ways of knowing, have been made at the lip of the abyss. There the phenomenologist as philosopher and poet keep company with the depth psychologists, with Freud and his ilk and especially with Jung, who has explored deeper layers of those depths.

48

OUT FROM UNDER THE COVERS

On the bridge that spans the abyss, on the bridge between the philosopher and the poet, I smile now with the recognition that psychology has been my cover story, a good cover for the wanderings I have done with those companions. And I smile because in some way that seems so right about the deeper currents of wisdom that guide our way, my wanderings seem to have been so much in accord with my name. Romanyshyn means "son of a gypsy", son of the "Roma", the people who are tricksters, vagabonds, musicians, story tellers, tellers of fortune, thieves, conjurers and, perhaps most important of all, orphans always on the journey home.

Here at the end I am again on a journey heralded by a dream, which for the past five years has been beckoning me toward another threshold. Here is the dream:

> In the dream I am in an old Victorian house and in a room of that house where many of my well suited and tied academic colleagues are standing in a circle. To them I am invisible and no words that I say seem to be heard by them. Wandering the house, I enter a middle room where a poet in shabby garb and with tobacco-stained teeth and fingers is with a young woman. He is about to introduce her to the secrets of poetry, especially the Orphic poets in the guise of Rilke. There is a distinct air of enlivening Eros in the atmosphere. They leave and I, feeling very much alone, begin to wander through the house again when I find myself at the back of it in the kitchen where the cooks are preparing food. The savory and rich aromas of the food are enticing and I notice how light and airy the room is, especially compared with the room where my colleagues are. A screen door through which the fresh breezes of a summer day enter opens to a field where I can see people picnicking on the grass, young lovers strolling hand-in-hand, and young children playing games. The field is full of life and laughter. Then I notice the poet is standing beside me. He opens the screen door and points to the field of life. The dream ends there on that threshold.

Like the dreams of long ago this one is like an oracle. Its symbols, especially the threshold, are ambiguous and require that sensibility that has no need to fix a meaning. I have been working with that dream and some clarity is beginning to emerge, but I will leave the hints of that direction unstated. However, in the spirit of this essay in praise to the humanities and the liberal arts I will end with this brief remark about time and the words of a poet that resonate with the spirit of the dream.

As there is no straight line of progress from one dream to the next, there is no straight line of progress in the humanities. In the same way that the dream I had last night is not an improvement on the dream I had last year, the paintings of Pollack, for example, are not an improvement on those of Giotto. But there are patterns. In our dream life these patterns are built on the ways in which each dream re-collects earlier dreams, returns to them, takes them up, preserves and transforms them. In the same fashion each age and each culture creates the stories and images that express and belong to a world and in so doing each age takes up what has already been created and fashions it anew. As Merleau-Ponty notes, the whole history of painting was already pre-figured in the caves at Lascaux.

In living life we live time not as a line from a dead past to an unborn future, but as a spiral where every present moment is a potential act of creation, where every present moment is ripe with a past, which in being re-membered imagines a future, and with a future, which in being imagined re-members a past. This potential is what makes us most human and it is what the humanities cultivate. In writing this essay in defense of the humanities, I am that boy who more than sixty years ago entered the library, that boy who later stole Freud from the library, and all those older versions of the pattern that I am and now the one again on a threshold. In my study they all live and the worlds in which they dwell are a living present.

We shall not cease from exploration
And the end of all our exploring
Will be to arrive where we started
And know the place for the first time. (Eliot 1943)

REFERENCES

Eliot, T. S. *Four Quartets*. 1954. New York: Harcourt Brace, 1971. 59, ll. 239-42.

Shakespeare, William. 1931/1969. "The Tempest." *William Shakespeare: The Complete Works*. Ed. Alfred Harbage. New York: Viking Press. 4.1.156-58.

Virgil. 1999. *The Aeneid, Book 6. Ecologues; Georgics; Aeneid I-VI*. Trans. H. R. Fairclough. Cambridge: Harvard U Press, 1999. ll. 126-29, 540-41.

PUTTING A FINGER ON OUR EDUCATION PROBLEM: A VETERAN ENGLISH PROFESSOR ADDS A LITERARY TOUCH

Paul Zolbrod

In struggling to deal with the nation's current educational decline, and more particularly with how it signals a growing reduction of humanities education today, I believe I can put my finger on a symptom, if not part of the cause. Or so I fancy by taking that hackneyed metaphor literally and pointing to a specific passage from an early American short story.

The work is Washington Irving's once celebrated but now overshadowed, "Legend of Sleepy Hollow." Some may recall his tale of Ichabod Crane, the itinerant schoolmaster who runs a small backwoods school in the upper Hudson Valley, and how he takes a fancy to Katrina Van Tassel, the comely daughter of a prosperous farmer, more for her father's wealth than for her beauty. Presuming he can win her by virtue of his status as a pedagogue and the mere fact that he wants to be her husband, he little suspects that his plan, together with his vanity, will be upended by his rival for her affection Brom Bones, disguised as a headless horseman, terrorizes him into superstitious flight. Those who know the story will recall the episode where Ichabod has been summoned to a harvest festival at the Van Tassel farm. Accepting the invitation as a go-ahead to propose to Katarina and win her, he makes his way confidently to the farm on a borrowed old nag. And as he approaches the house, he takes inventory of its riches, smugly considering the estate as good as his:

> As Ichabod jogged slowly on his way, his eye, ever open to every symptom of culinary abundance, ranged with delight over the treasures of jolly autumn. On all sides he beheld a vast store of apples; some

hanging in oppressive opulence on the trees; some gathered into baskets and barrels for the market; others heaped up in rich piles for the cider-press. Farther on he beheld great fields of Indian corn, with its golden ears peeping from their leafy coverts, and holding out the promise of cakes and hasty pudding; and the yellow pumpkins lying beneath them, turning up their fair round bellies to the sun, and giving ample prospects of the most luxurious of pies, and anon he passed the fragrant buckwheat fields, breathing the odor of the bee-hives, and as he beheld them, soft anticipations stole over his mind of dainty slap-jacks, well buttered, and garnished with honey or treacle, by the delicate little dimpled hand of Katrina Van Tassel. (Irving 1983, 1074-75)

With its vivid imagery buttressed by a subtle poetic cadence, the passage evokes a visual impression of Ichabod's horse ambling up to the farmhouse as he looks around. Readers can envision his approach and grasp his foolishly premature sense of ownership. Observe not so much the passage's entire sentences, but its measured phrases; or better still, imagine hearing them as they list detail upon opulent detail. With the exception of the opening sentence and the closing independent clause, each separate phrase contains a nearly uniform number of syllables in a slow paced rhythm that underscores his gathering awareness of what he sees.

Thus with print as his medium, Irving helps the reader see, not just with robust images, but with measured phrasing. Or so I reflected one recent fall as I reviewed "The Legend of Sleepy Hollow" for an early American literature class I was teaching at a small regional state university in the mountain Southwest. A relevant point, I thought, worth making to students steeped in the virtual reality of the movie screen or video monitor. Thanks to the passage's visual and auditory sharpness, when reading it myself I tend to imagine the action in movie-like scenes, and wondered whether students did as well. Simple enough—or so I thought, expecting that the connection would make for an interesting discussion.

To my dismay, however, it did not. Instead they sat silently, some perched behind laptops, others with Blackberries and smart phones at their fingertips, seemingly indifferent to my suggestion. When I challenged their non-response, without exception they admitted that they had not read the story, claiming it was too hard. "Anyhow, I don't have to read it," one of them declared while others nodded, not so much defensively as in defiance: "I saw the movie, and Johnny Depp was in it!" Who needs to read the story when Depp acts it out on the screen in a version replete with Hollywood-Gothic special effects?

Taking the course to satisfy a humanities requirement, they had been struggling with the material, more committed to their battery-driven gadgets than to Columbus's letters from the New World, Gaspar Pérez de Villlagrá's epic account of the Spanish colonization of the upper Rio Grande Valley, Anne Bradstreet's Puritan musings on childbirth and homemaking in the Massachusetts wilderness, Jonathan Edwards's sermon on "Sinners in the Hands of an Angry God," or Alexander Hamilton's doctrine, in Federalist No. 1, of separate states united by duly elected representatives. In past years as the syllabus gave way to more accessible writers like Irving, students began warming up to the material. What has changed, though, since the advent of notepads, smart phones, and other portable electronic devices, is an open resistance to the printed page. Now students do not read, or they come to class declaring texts too difficult for their abilities.

That avowal in itself is not necessarily new at a regional, open admissions university with a predominantly Hispanic and Native American student body, which to me is especially perplexing. More and more frequently I either hear it outright, or experience it tacitly when students arrive in class unprepared. After teaching at a selective liberal arts college back east for thirty years, I welcomed the post-retirement challenge of sharing with minority, first-generation college students the pleasure of mastering early American literature, but increasingly I feel the effects of a generational divide in how literacy now applies as an agent of the humanities. Or rather how it does not.

The son of immigrants, I began my childhood in working class Pittsburgh during the depression, wearing hand-me-downs, walking everywhere because we had no car, expecting to live out my adulthood working in a mill or a coal mine, or to follow my father into the freight yards, much like other kids in my neighborhood. Just the same, almost entirely by way of print we were all getting a fairly standard public school education, which among other things initiated us into the humanities without our being aware of it. Still strong, my schoolboy recollections include reading Longfellow's "The Courtship of Miles Standish" and "Evangeline," Cooper's *The Last of the Mohicans*, Hawthorne's *House of the Seven Gables* and *The Scarlet Letter*, poems and prose works by Emerson, Whitman, Whittier, Melville, and Emily Dickinson, along with British standards like Shakespeare, Milton, and Pope; Coleridge, Wordsworth, Byron, Shelley and Keats; Browning, Tennyson, Dickens, and the Bronte sisters—writers whom today many of my students have never read, let alone heard of—all without movie versions or film strips at that time. History likewise came from books almost exclusively.

As a result, related images were ours to imagine; the ideas and impressions were ours as well to process and grapple with, helped by teachers whose own primary medium was print. Why that matters as I look back now is that while many of us were first generation Americans whose parents brought with them old country ways, we were acquiring an American identity, which virtually sanctified the Declaration of Independence, the Bill of Rights, the Constitution, and selections from the *Federalist Papers*, which we also absorbed from the page. Therein lays the essence of the American Dream as I remember coming to sense it—not in today's more narrowly and crassly materialistic notion of a house and a car and a steady job, but as a common identity in a national experiment. All of it was ours to grasp without so much as a hint that acquiring a taste for literature made for elitism, or that there would eventually be a distinction between highbrow, middlebrow and lowbrow culture. This was to be our country, and we were absorbing its values largely by way of print, sometimes with a graphic boost from *Life* Magazine or *National Geographic* and Saturday matinee movies, but without the now-familiar glare of video screen or PowerPoint. Yes, there were serious exclusions in a curriculum heavily patriarchal, blind to an African American cultural legacy, a Native viable tradition, and a Hispanic presence older than the Anglo Saxon one. They would be overcome, however, as part of Martin Luther King, Jr.'s stirring vision of that dream. More essentially, as new perspectives on American society emerged, our training as readers helped us internalize them. Presumably we were poised to look critically at the past and revise our views not by passively processing electronically mounted sound bites that stir the emotions more readily than the mind, but by reasoning actively as we had learned as readers to do. Nostalgic for such a time, I still wish to impart the best of those ideals to the students I now teach, which I believe is essential if we are to save our democracy and preserve our humanity.

As luck would have it, I made it to college and transcended my working class moorings, thanks to the G. I. Bill, which had further democratized colleges and universities, and thanks all the more to the way I had learned to master print without the electronic distractions students now must overcome—if I may put it that way. And that's what I wanted those students to consider when I raised the question about how they envisioned Ichabod Crane's entrance into a world of pastoral affluence. Openly wondering whether their minds operated differently now that electronic media filled the brain, I hoped to get them to marvel about how Irving could transmit so vivid an experience with a technology so rudimentary as the written word, without so much as a typewriter or even a ballpoint pen to put letters on a page one at a time.

Thus "The Legend of Sleepy Hollow" occupies an important place in my syllabus. Now largely overlooked as a serious literary work, it continues to appear in textbooks as "one of America's best loved stories." Its playful gothic backdrop can make it fun to read and discuss in a classroom setting; and while undervalued, it marks the entry of American literature onto the world stage, given Irving's growing reputation across the Atlantic, which I like to emphasize to these non-mainstream students. With its apparent light-heartedness, it invites wide interpretation as an American short story composed at a crucial time in the nation's early past. It can be read as a benchmark account of an educated Yankee misfit in a backwoods community, of a conniving opportunist driven away by shrewd farm folk, or of a callow outsider greedy to insinuate himself in a simple farm community. The rootless Ichabod could represent a young country searching for a national identity. By making a local legend a catalyst for its outcome, the story might also stand as a search for a mythic past independent of Europe's. On the other hand, it can be taken as an indictment of book learning in a newly formed republic where practical knowledge matters more. Or as the story of a guileless, superstitious fool expelled by a headless horseman, it can suggest an equally foolish retreat into the world of the imagination.

Because the possibilities seem endless, I ask students to develop a studied reading of their own. I want them to look closely not just *at* a text, but *into* it for their own discovered interpretation. Given that institution's demographics, I use such an exercise to promote the centrality of reading and writing to learning, even if digital technology appears to be supplanting the conventional page. Beyond assigning works that evoke awareness their own ethnic past, I want them to connect more securely with a mainstream culture that allows for a grand mosaic of clashing ideas. While print has declined as a medium of choice, I believe its mastery should matter to them, not only as a primary educational tool, but as an empowering one that gives them, too, a place in that variegated social scheme.

In so saying, I invoke not only the microcosm of my own Early American literature classroom at a regionally unique state university. I am speaking more universally, inasmuch as the resistance to reading is happening in the broader context of educational decline. According to one widely embraced survey, 32 percent of recent college graduates surveyed did not take a single course which required 40 pages of reading and 50 pages of writing, and on average studied no more than 13 hours weekly, or less than half the time their 1960 counterparts spent studying. At a time of grade inflation when students see themselves as clients and consumers, 36 percent of those who say they spent five hours or less studying graduated with a G.P.A. of 3.16 (Arum and Roska 2011). That last figure comes as no surprise to me when most in my students openly expect to receive at least a "B," irrespective of the work they intend doing. Yet soon they will join fellow graduates elsewhere in evaluating issues like climate change, or the subtle pros and cons of a corporate-driven global economy—not according to carefully drawn inferences from well-written arguments, but from Twitter-length bytes or talk-show shouting matches.

To what extent does digital technology explain the overall decline in literary skills we are witnessing more often today, if indeed that is what it is, especially now that new media are being so roundly embraced by the educational establishment? The May 8, 2011 issue of *The Chronicle of Higher Education*, seen by many as the academic community's official trade journal, devoted an entire section to the digitalization of the campus. With titles like "Stanford U.'s Grand Experiment," "Info Tech on Campuses: By the Numbers," and "Teaching Paperless Writing," most articles in it praise techniques for adapting the iPad, Twitter, Facebook, and smart phones into classroom instruction. Meanwhile, a scant few urge caution or tend toward outright skepticism. As for me, I want to accept the new technology with an open mind, even though I now belong to a shrinking minority nostalgic for a time when papers were typed manually on a standard typewriter, chalk was a classroom mainstay, and students went to the library reference desk or retreated alone into the stacks to locate source material.

In reading those *Chronicle* articles, I noticed frequent reference to collaborative learning. Not in itself a bad thing, but its growing acceptance could signal a turning away from meditative study. Ironically, the wireless technology and the Internet alike summon us to the screen, but mostly in acts of social networking or reliance on a prefabricated database in place of a self-initiated search. Thus it seems that learning is increasingly done in tandem with others rather than independently, especially as services like Twitter and Facebook beckon students and teachers to gather online, while technology-based group activities have become more frequent in the classroom. Consider this possibility, however: cyberspace is public and crowded, while reading is private and solitary. Moreover, its mirror image, writing, ultimately requires one's deepest reflection before it can, and perhaps should, be shared.

As *The New York Times* executive editor Bill Keller suggests in the May 22nd, 2011 issue of its Sunday magazine, the reliance on Google and MySpace or the likes of Twitter and YouTube can disrupt the kind of contemplative self-reflection that reading promotes. Thus I bring this pair of questions to the reduced practice and its probably concomitant educational decline. In settling for simple assertions or wresting small bytes of data from a broader context, what becomes of one's own interpretative capacity? And what ramifications does the union of educational technology with social media bring to the practice of reading in solitude?

In my estimation, solitary reading remains central to real classroom success. Recognized long before the advent of the printing press, its transportive power funnels all the senses uniquely inward. As early as the fourth century, Augustine in his *Confessions* observed that while reading scripture, a fellow churchman's eyes "went over the pages and his heart looked into the sense," while "voice and tongue were resting" (Augustine 2011, 102). Likewise, print's capacity for speaking silently calls for an exclusively internalized focus, leaving the mind itself to build its own imagined reality independent of all the senses. It liberates the individual from the constraints of space and time through a process of self-reliance that leads to an altered awareness of the immediate present. My colleague, Dennis Patrick Slattery at Pacifica Graduate Institute, where I have also taught following my retirement from Allegheny College, writes that when elevated to poetry, reading can provide a kind of knowledge "unavailable any other way through any other discipline" (Slattery 2008, 6). And the great historian of religion, Mircea Eliade, claims that by way of the printed page, a reader "succeeds in obtaining an escape from time" to "live in another 'history'" (1987, 205).

In fifty years of teaching, I have come to accept that quality as fundamental to learning—from the inside out, as it were, so that the aware self becomes the launching pad for acknowledging and responding to what happens externally. Whether in its broadest sense as all that is written or as a narrowly academic discipline of interpreting passages from Shakespeare or Jane Austin, literature is central to the educational mission, all the more so, I believe, now that the senses are literally bombarded to the extent that a special effects explosion on the giant screen becomes an omnipresent metaphor, leaving us all vulnerable to misinformation and distortion in defiance of our most deeply reflecting selves.

That intrusive reality is why I believe students should take singular refuge in the "twittering blackbirds flying in sable clouds" (Irving 1983, 1074) Ichabod Crane sees on his way to the Van Tassel household, and to reflect carefully when he chuckles self-indulgently "with the possibility that he might one day be lord of all this scene . . . " (ibid., 1076). This is so especially at the present time when I find the country at greater risk than I have ever been aware of, not from outside threats, as was true with WWII or the Cold War, but from within the country by circumstances of our own making. I wish, therefore, that students could learn better to travel inward, where in Walt Whitman's terms, they can loaf and invite their souls. As a seasoned college teacher whose gaze inevitably returns to the individual student, my own ongoing deep learning originates in the solitude of looking up a word in the dictionary, constantly reexamining the system known as grammar that makes a language work—struggling to break a dense sentence down into clauses, reducing them to subjects and main verbs along with their modifiers whether adjectives or adverbs, be they individual words or as entire phrases. Yes, I still do that, and in so doing I find myself entertaining this question, not rhetorically as if the answer is obviously at hand but openly, as wired and wireless engagement with a screen increases more on behalf of commerce and consumerism than as a champion of the examined life. Does the electronic reality that technology now delivers promote engagement with the humanities, or does it erode that essential dimension of the educational mission?

Such deliberation can lead a young reader to see that Ichabod Crane might have known better; he should have admitted to himself that his attraction to Katrina and her father's farm was not an honest one. Or in wonder and growing awareness, that kind of concerted attention may yield some alternate conclusion. In either case, the dynamic is ongoing, as it should be in an educational setting, where one measured reading gives way to another, as I get to experience when a student's fresh perspective alters my own seasoned interpretation. It is no overstatement to say that minds thus interact across a generational divide in ways not possible on Facebook or email or Twitter, where hasty reaction preempts reasoned reflection, and the power of one's own interpretive imagination is lost. Never mind, then, whether today's sought-after educational reform is a matter of competing in a world market to promote consumerism, much as Ichabod Crane evidently wished to become a consumer rather than a working farmer. Ask instead if it meets an abiding need to build on the best that has been thought and said.

Or does that question no longer apply in an educational setting where screen and keyboard dominate, and learning satisfies only the marketplace and one's own appetite to partake of it? That, of course, is a rhetorical question, and brings me back to Washington Irving's image of Ichabod Crane's approach to the Van Tassel farmhouse. Read it again in its overall context not just of the story but of young America's emergence in pursuit of a new Athenian ideal. Unlike my students, feast on each phrase and listen to the voice it transmits. Notice how there it is the medium of print that feeds the brain with images only the mind can produce for one's own self—which completes the circuit that secures the connection between individual alphabetical units and pictures that emanate from within. Isn't that where our awareness of what it is to be human internalizes?

As what might remain the greatest technology of all, it is still an alphabet that reduces meaningful human sounds to visible signs and transmits them across the barriers of time and space. As for digital units, they function only as electronic surrogates—and with this corrupting effect: they convert the replicated voice to refabricated sounds and ready-made pictures at the expense of reading with one's own inner voice where the old stories are heard more directly. Or so I learned before miniature screens could be carried in pocket or purse, digital bytes shorted out a durable connection between writer and reader far more direct than a screen now allows, and the wonderful introspection that raw print still invites became overwhelmed.

REFERENCES

Arum, Richard, and Josipa Roksa. 2011. *Academically Adrift: Limited Learning on College Campuses.* Chicago: U of Chicago Press.

Eliade, Mircea. 1987. *The Sacred and the Profane: The Nature of Religion.* Trans. Willard R. Trask. Orlando: Harcourt.

Irving, Washington. 1983. "The Legend of Sleepy Hollow." In *History, Tales, and Sketches.* New York: Library of America, 1983.

St. Augustine. 2001. *The Confessions of Saint Augustine.* Trans. Rex Warner. New York: Penguin.

Slattery, Dennis. 2008. "Dante's Terza Rima in *The Divine Comedy:* The Road of Therapy." *International Journal of Transpersonal Studies* 27: 80-90.

THE HUMANITIES TAKE A WALK OUTSIDE TIME

Kathryn LaFevers Evans

Hail to you, ye lords of endless recurrence and establishers of changelessness.
Seize not my heart with your fingers in this year (or) in this month; seize not this heart.
May ye not make up your mind(s) on the basis of any evil words (spoken) against me,
for[,] as for this heart of mine
it is the great heart that is in the Ogdoad.
The great god whose words are in the members of him,
he sends (his) heart out of his body,
that my heart may become more inventive than (those of) the gods.
~Egyptian Book of the Dead

This great heart that is in the Ogdoad—that my heart may become more inventive—is the heart of academia known as the humanities. Yes, the sciences and business are the strong skeleton of our collective body made of knowledge, but the humanities is our deep heart made of wisdom. I know this to be true from experience, even in just this short half-a-century lifetime: that the heart of education carries our imaginations outside of our own time, so that we can know the timeless value of our collective past and present as well as for our shared future. The humanities, through the language of epic poetry and other mythologies, open our minds to that timeless great heart of humanity, so that we can invent—can co-create—the best possible future for humankind.

We, as humanities teachers and students, constitute history walking beyond the walls of Bibles. The Coffin Text above belonged to a specific people in Egypt, and was buried at a specific time in the antiquity of human history. Why is it, then, that we can exhume this text long dead and buried,

61

to find within its words deep human meaning that transcends time? Why is it that I would spend my lifetime mining the ancient deserts of human words for wisdom out of which I can invent a new story today, for you readers today and in the future? It is because part of humanity's reality is that our souls do transcend space and time through self-reflection and study of the deep heart. We like, indeed we need, to reflect on the meaning of human life. We need to share our hearts in words throughout time, one to another, as if we could walk beyond the walls of Bibles and speak to each beyond the walls of time—to each other—in a common language of universal human truths.

I agree that mathematics may be the common language of the universe; it's very exact, the true blueprint. That's a "given" precept in academia today, along with a now-loudly-vocalized wish that the humanities would just take a hike. And it seems also to be the general consensus that if we hope to ever communicate in a common language with people outside of our race and from distant worlds, it may well be through mathematics, yes. But, what is it that we will have to say to them? What is it in the human heart that may be of value and meaning to them?

Whatever that value is, the same must be true amongst humanity today: that the essence of humanity is borne through time on the wings of human words that capture even the ineffable within the walls of myth. Through mythic imagination we invent and co-create our future together. What has become of the great heart, the great myth of human freedom achieved by our ancestors when we claimed that right for the United States of America just over 200 years ago? Who will be there in future generations to stand and tell the mythologies taught in the humanities to the children as they grow from infancy, through adolescence, and into adulthood? That great heart of the humanities in academia, whether at the kindergarten level or the doctoral level, still beats within each of us alive today. Society at large receives the wisdom that blossoms out of the humanities, because wisdom walks beyond the walls of institutions. So we are equipped to tell that story, to share that mythic reality of freedom with our fellow humans worldwide. Egypt is an example in point this year, 2011: because of the educated free world at large broadcasting the reality of freedom via the Internet, Egyptians and other oppressed citizens worldwide are continuing to claim that freedom which is the birthright of every human.

FREEDOM: A TIMELESS HUMAN MYTH

May Heaven be thy joy, may the Abyss [Ía] . . .

May the gods of the world be favourable to thee: may the great gods bless thy heart!
May Ía increase thy dominion!
O Damkina, lady of heaven and earth!
—Babylonian & Assyrian incantations & magical formulae

Egypt is free, as of February 11th 2011. An ancient people, an ancient civilization, in self-captivity all of those thousands of years—waiting for our voice, waiting to hear their own voice ring with ours clear and sweet for freedom, for peace. Did that one day end the turmoil of social reorganization? No, of course not. And this year as well it's plain to see that American freedom is a continuous, daily commitment by each citizen to claim freedom. It is an idea, an ideal, a very palpable reality within the *anima mundi* or soul of the world, which we each fight for, truly, every day in our very individual ways. America's President Barack Obama said of Egypt's freedom: "There's something in the soul that cries out for freedom." Can any more be said for the value of humankind's myths to bring us continually into a better future? Only 200 years ago Americans told each other that myth, spread the myth, shared the myth of freedom; peoples around the world have been re-telling that mythology of human freedom in all languages since then; and before that, throughout time to the beginning of our remembrance of being human—our remembrance of being. There is no deeper soul from which to be perpetually reborn, re-invented, than the hidden chamber of the human heart. The humanities is an essential conduit for the expression of heart out into the greater world.

HEART BEING FROM THE TIMELESS ONE

The Primal One: the Soul sees and in its emotion
tries to represent what it sees and breaks into speech
'on—-einai—-ousia—-hestia'
([Being] Existent; Existence; Essence; Hestia or Hearth [Heart-Sun]),
sounds which labor to express the essential nature of the being
produced by the travail of the utterer and so to represent, as far as sounds may,
the origin of reality.
—*Plotinus: The Enneads, 5.5.5*

The wanderings of the human heart . . . the adytum or hidden chamber of our shared human body-temple . . . We are all out of Africa; our hearts share the same blood of the ancestors from 6 million years ago; humanity is of One soul. How is it that, at the turn of a new millennium, 300 Egyptians who died for the freedom of their countrymen today, have become immortalized within our shared human myth for all time? How is it that millions of people around the world stood by them, as they presented themselves without armor, naked to their armed countrymen? And how is it that we all, together, were able to withstand the threat of violence, knew how to stand by them in peace like we have for so many millennia in war? It is because we have already begun the work of telling ourselves, teaching each other, a new myth, a new mythology of human peace for our global future. The human race is arguably only now maturing out of our infancy into adolescence. During this adolescence we have begun to tell ourselves the story of how we are responsible enough now to clean up after ourselves, to take turns, and to share resources peacefully with each other. Though there may still be bloodshed now and in our future, through looking back in time and learning—through educating ourselves in the humanities—we have come to know that it is a shared destiny we are writing, inventing, co-creating. And it is in our own best interest to go about our lives peacefully as we walk together beyond the walls of Bibles. The Egyptian civilians of our time stood and faced their armed countrymen, pouring out their hearts to them: "The people and the military are One." Muslims called out to their countrymen, "Islam and Christianity are One."

These are cries from deep within the human heart of our soul. But, what is it really that we're after? What kind of freedom? Along with freedom from exterior oppressions, it's also inner freedom that our soul is crying out for, isn't it? Each of us wants to find out for ourselves what really makes us tick, what our individual authentic Self, the heart of our soul, truly is. We want the freedom to think for ourselves, and discovering what that truly means is an inborn right. A true university offers, within fully developed programs and majors, the full range of human endeavors. The core, *coeur*, or heart of human endeavor is the spiritual inspiration, the emotion of awe we feel, at being in the world. Humans transform that inspiration into ritual, and into the mythologies by which we will remember, forever, to celebrate the One heart that beats in our soul. Human inspiration, co-creation, invention is our existent being that emanates out from our One heart; it's from out of this spirit that we walk within ritual and we breathe within myth. This work of the humanities is our soul's body and breath, its Primal One.

Our educational systems from infancy, through adolescence, through adulthood and on into lifetime learning, must engage this human work of mythology, our archetypal legacy to the future of humankind. Within the academy and in clinical practice worldwide, psychology is the science of the human mind and soul. The soul cries out for freedom, seeks self-

64

transformation, and freedom from self-bondage in ignorance. Depth and archetypal psychology teach us to invent, to co-create the world through archetypal imagination and myth, from the depths of that esoteric hidden realm within the One human heart. And these educational disciplines guide us to those universal human values that in ethical, moral ways will change the world for the better, for all of humankind—"forever," as President Obama said of Egypt's freedom. Every day, each of us continues to bring freedom from within our individuality, out to our communities, nations, and world.

THE TIME MACHINE

The Sun more true measureth all things by time,
being itself the time of time,
according to the Oracle of the Gods concerning it.
—Proclus in Timaeus, 249. Z. or T.
The Chaldean Oracles of Zoroaster, fragment 131

Nihil novi sub sole. There is nothing new under the sun. It is through living the mythologies of our individual mortal body in time, written with the blood of our human heart through past and present, that our future is known. It is through time spent in darkness that we come to value the heart of our soul as the light-giving sun itself. I'll tell you a story of how I know this to be true.

In the year 1997 "of our Lord" as some American politicians this year would confine time—the year I had come to know, through higher education, in a more universal sense as 1997 CE, of the "Common Era"— I graduated from a 17-year course of self-study known as Raja Yoga, the Royal Road. This was as Jungian Studies are—an introspective study of the individual soul and mind, for the sake of soul-making and tending the *anima mundi*, soul of the world.

In 1973 I had graduated from high school in a rural coastal community in Southern California . . . yes, such were the times that parts of the Southern California coastline were still rural. As the 1973 Carpinteria High School valedictorian, I had nothing to say, for my speech in that year of Watergate, in that era of Vietnam, would have only been bitter, with no words of wisdom to offer my fellow graduates. I could not write a speech that opened onto a brighter future for America. The time of my life was that of idealism in despair, and I knew only how to protest, not how to guide. My future was wide open: I could have become an exotic scientist of botany or astronomy, discovering the primordial powers of the sun; or a mathematician, biologist, or physicist calculating the elemental powers of the sun to regenerate humankind; but instead I chose to study the human story in myth, literature, poetry to find out what it was, ultimately, that makes us human. And I found, speaking for myself, that the seat of the soul is not in the human intellect, but in the human heart—something larger than life that binds us together in a shared destiny.

In 1997, I came back, after a quarter of a century, to visit the teacher at Carpinteria High School who had taught my heart the mythic poetry of Spenser, Yeats, and Ovid, and the mythopoetic drama of Shakespeare—Mr. Baird, the English teacher. Mr. Baird, the Bard of Avon, yes mythopoetically Shakespeare himself, like the timepiece of time itself, still teaching, still ticking.

When I stepped across that threshold of my past, it was mid-afternoon, at just the time when the cheerleaders gathered by the quad to practice, and the football-basketball-baseball players jostled past them on their way to the gym for after-school practice. And there to greet me, lording over the cheerleaders, was King Jock, Hero of the School, looking directly at me to make sure I recognized just who he was. Yes of course I do, my eyes reassured him; but you're nothing to me, an outgrown shell really. And in that recognition of the archetype, as I stepped across the threshold from the parking lot onto campus, I could feel the wounded hero within me slough off like a lizard's skin, making way for a more interior self-image. I pressed on past the cheerleaders, contemporary incarnations of my past. They were the same as we had been. Our generation of Flower Children had spawned a new generation, Children of the Crystal, or some such myth. I passed by, across the sidewalk that spanned the campus' central lawn, renewed with a sense of forgiveness, of peace. They were the same ones—are the same ones, circling round again in their turn. And then the trees planted along the sidewalk leading across the lawn: they had been saplings then—now full-grown trees. Time had passed, like a miracle, revealing the meaning of mystery, of awe, that I had been fed with all of these years: the magic of words, of myth, of walking through time as my own myth unfolded.

I had not set foot on that small campus in my hometown, just down the street from my parents' home, for 24 years. And what I noticed was that the trees had grown, so very big from the saplings I sat under in those days, eating my lunch with friends. How could that be, that they had grown so? That much time had passed; it was written in their trunks, limbs, and leaves—that time could not be undone. It was so. And so had been the growth of my life, day by day, leaf by leaf. Slowly, imperceptibly, in time with nature's passing, I had grown. So that now, a quarter of a century later, I could write that valedictorian's speech—the one I was meant to give all along, having only to wait for the growth of my limbs, natural, with the passage of time. I needed to write it for my nephew, the first-born of my brothers, who had come to our wedding in his 6-year-old three piece suit, looking ever so much like he did in later years, only smaller: for the new generation of children of the sun, I had to write it. There was only one step left to take in order to tell them a story worthy of our future; one step left, for me to go back in time and get her—the girl that had fallen from Eden with the flood of Watergate in 1973.

I crossed the threshold of my English teacher's classroom. Yes, the same classroom he had taught in 24 years before, when I had graduated, when I had been looking to see if he had come to my rite of passage. But no. I hadn't passed the ritual: my soul hadn't ripened even to that, a simple high school graduation, a Vietnam, a Watergate. So after college, after one failed engagement, a failed marriage, after this second marriage, and career, and children . . . I went back to get her. And she met me, my soul, in that English teacher's classroom, and wept with me for the years past, for the girl who had come so far, and the brave teacher who had stood his ground for more than a quarter of a century, and would go on still, teaching. He is my true hero, the one I thought of those long winters at college in the snow, the deep, white, silent snow. My inspiration, my muse—that's all, a simple miracle, a teacher whose job it was to share humankind's great works, epic myths of great heart. Shakespeare, Spenser, Whitman, Homer, Ovid—the Egg, the Womb of Creation, nothing less.

I had been a math tutor during high school. It was easy for me; I enjoyed teaching my peers how to work the proofs. I had been a bright light, the dean said, and he had wondered what I had made of my life. No, I didn't choose the language of math and physics, though they were second nature. I chose my own first nature, which was that language of human words I had been born into: English. What a miracle that is: 99% of our genetic make-up is identical to chimpanzees, but their vocalized language is rudimentary compared to humankind's range of expression through language. For me, nothing compares to the transformational process of clothing naked human words in mythology. It is the deepest secret, before silence. Some say that numbers are the final form before silence; for me it is words, which like a whispered veil, open my soul to the ground of silence. No words can thank my high school English teacher for having been there for me when my soul needed to learn what it meant to be human; for being there still, all those years; for standing his ground with no armor in the face of a hard-shelled enemy—the teenage psyche. No acts can repay the kindness freely given; except perhaps to write the myth of the wounded hero, the little girl who grew up.

So this is how the story goes. After choosing. Choosing to study humankind's story, what it means to be human, mortal, tragically flawed, comically driven. After choosing humanities over the sciences or business, I earned my Bachelor's degree in Comparative Literature and Research in Consciousness from a school out of time, in the field of dreams, in the cornfields of Iowa. I could not have survived this mortal life in Berkeley—that was my choice, though I had no other, in truth. Narrow is the way—you know that to be true, I'm sure of it. This is our story, our human story.

So, after college and a failed engagement, a failed marriage, and then a sweet, sweet marriage with the fruit of two children—a quarter of a century after my undergraduate studies—I needed to go back in time again to get her.

I applied to Cal State San Marcos, during a deep depression in the winter of 2002. My husband was working there to help build the new campus, and this was a "perk" offered to spouses. I had kept on in my studies of course, accompanying my children to a Sunday school, according to our own faith. And we mothers met, while the children were learning, and we read the words of a teacher who, for us, was a personal God. Yes, that can be so, sometimes—a God alive in our lifetime; and this time it was so for us. And it was during one of those readings that she instructed me, "Get the degree." Yes, those were her very words. No looking back; only going forwards, into my own future. Where it would lead I did not know. She had been speaking, my God, on the unity of religions; but I could not attend on that weekend because of family obligations. But I knew I could attend to her during school hours, while the children were cared for and my husband at work. I threw caution to the wind, writing in my Literature & Writing Studies graduate application mission statement, that I wanted to study names and symbols of God. Well, since there was no Religious Studies Department on this new campus yet, and since only three philosophy courses were offered, the Literature & Writing Studies department decided that I would be a good addition to other students enrolling in their graduate program that year. Imagine that.

I entered graduate studies in the summer of 2002, with my first course Sacred Texts taught by a Medieval Studies professor. She was brutal, and just the thing to drag us raw through Dante's *Inferno*, with no time in the course for *Purgatorio*, much less *Paradiso*. That was her way—the way of pain. She showed us clearly her pain, her wish that we could step out of our cloistered lives and minds to see the pain of the world, the inequities of our system of higher education, the fact that we must be able to speak the profane in academia in order to earn the gift of teaching the sacred. She was very direct. This was all very clear. And I thought, "You've shown us your pain, now show us your bliss. I feel it inside you, buried deep down through the masculine rigors of academic training, dying to be heard, dying to re-invent you, to be born as a new way of teaching."

I had a kindred spirit in that Sacred Texts class, an American Zen Buddhist about my age. He had returned for a master's degree in Business, in order to make a living in the world, and had chosen Sacred Texts as an elective, unbeknownst to him under the tutelage of a recovering Catholic professor of Medieval Studies. He wore a Buddhist talisman of sorts around his neck, so we all knew he was of the East. We sat across the room from each other, but often shared a like mind of commenting to the teacher and class how, in the Eastern religions, such and such a wisdom is known, which, clearly, you are telling us is not to be found in the Western tradition. You have shown us our pain, clearly. . . And myself my own anger, over the failure of the Protestant church to soothe me as a child, to guide me, to show me my own bliss. But finally, after a good many weeks of agreeing with us—since she too was clearly angry at The Church for having slighted her, for having maimed her sisters in the time of the Inquisition—the teacher finally came to it, in response to the Buddhist and me: "But we have those mysteries too."

With those six words the teacher had exposed the rawness of my long years of anger directed at our Western Church, had exposed this only to myself of course—this was my personal epic myth; each of my fellow students had their own story to write. You've shown me your pain, I thought, our pain; now show me your bliss—that is, after all, what is required of you as a true teacher of Humanity.

So then one day, the day we had come to the gruesome end of our *Inferno*, she spoke the final words of the final Canto to us, gently and almost with her eyes closed, in Italian: "E quindi uscimmo a riveder le stele."

"It was from there that we emerged, to see—once more—the stars."

There, I thought, there is your bliss. Thank you, thank you my teacher. Release your pain, and come with the children of light, to the stars.

WE NEED THE GOLD OF THE SUN

The sacrifice has been accomplished: the divine child, the image of the God's formation, is slain, and I have eaten from the sacrificial flesh. The child, that is, the image of the God's formation, not only bore my human craving, but also enclosed all the primordial and elemental powers that the sons of the sun possess as an inalienable inheritance. The God needs all this for his genesis. But when he has been created and hastens away into unending space, we need the gold of the sun. We must regenerate ourselves. But as the creation of a God is a creative act of highest love, the restoration of our human life signifies an act of the Below. This is a great and dark mystery. [. . .] The primordial force is the radiance of the sun, which the sons of the sun have carried in themselves for aeons and pass on to their children.

—C .G. Jung, *The Red Book*

And what of the Zen Buddhist Business student in 2002, you ask? Well, here is what happened to him, to us.

Our paths crossed outside the library one day, and I asked him how the university's master's program in Business was going for him. He said it was brutal, likening it to our gruesome trip through the *Inferno*, with no path offered for the way out. He said they taught him that business is cut-throat; that's the way it's done, and the way it should be done.

Then in 2008, the US experienced an economic collapse. You know the rest of the story.

Much of what it means to be human has been recorded in the oral tradition, on stone, and in other forms of written texts, and through the arts of painting, sculpture, music, and dance, over millennia. The spiritual depths of the human soul are at the core of our One, mythopoetic heart. So the shared heart that's taught from generation to generation through the humanities is where we will find our true sense of One-ness, of peace. Humanity's self-reflective gaze, directed inward towards the heart, is practiced through the study of mythology along with depth and archetypal psychology, in the humanities. We are continually re-inventing ourselves through mythology: the science of how to read and practice the human heart. Mythology portrays and interprets deep archetypes common to humankind, drawing them with us through the ages, reinterpreting and applying them to new situations. Mythology, whether of giants or of quarks, records the essence of human history unfolding through the archetypes.

So, as we communicate globally in cyberspace, through a single web that is bound to each of us separately in our homes—as we communicate in many different human languages—we lift each other up out of our shared past in Africa, into a global freedom shared with contemporary Egyptians, and with Babylonians who are now contemporary Iranians, and with contemporary Africans, healed heroes from within the dark continent of our shared past. It is not through our clever theorems or calculations, but through the human mythopoesis of collective, archetypal mythologies, and through continually re-inventing a unified humanity out of our shared human heart, that we co-create freedom and peace in our time.

That we co-create peace outside time, in the realm of human imagination.

REFERENCES

Egyptian Book of the Dead, BD 27a S 2. Retrieved from http://oi.uchicago.edu/research/pubs/catalog/oip/oip82.html (accessed January 12, 2011).

Jung, C. G. 2009. "The Sacrificial Murder." *The Red Book*. New York: W. W. Norton & Company., 91, 291.

King, Leonard W. 1896/2010. *Babylonian Magic and Sorcery*. 1896. LaVergne, TN: BiblioLife, 2010, 24.

Plotinus: The Enneads.1992. Trans. Stephen MacKenna. New York: Larson Publications.

Westcott, William Wynn. 2008. *The Chaldean Oracles of Zoroaster*. Trans. Thomas Taylor and I. P. Cory. Lexington, KY: Forgotten Books.

AGITATING WAKEFULNESS: THE POWER OF THE HUMANITIES' PRESENCE

Dennis Patrick Slattery, Ph.D.

Why, if man can by patience select variations most useful to himself, should nature fail in selecting variations useful, under changing conditions of life, to her living products?
~Charles Darwin, *Origin of Species, 1859*

I could not have been older than 9 or 10 when I discovered that I had a bit of talent for the sleight of health. Whenever school became too dull, I would, early in the morning, wait in the bathroom and listen for my mother to pass by the door. As she came up the stairs after preparing breakfast and was about to pass the bathroom, I would begin to retch and pour water from a cup into the toilet to simulate vomiting. I knew she would hear this and open the door to check on me. I had already flushed the toilet so there was no residue of my contrived illness. But I had the ability to will a pathetic visage that seemed to satisfy her.

I knew that if I were successful in my role, she would allow me to stay home; perhaps she knew my shenanigans and wanted the company—I cannot say for certain. What I was sure of is that she would go to the public library in Euclid, Ohio and bring back 10 or so books for me and several for herself. I do believe watching her reading in as many spare minutes as she could muster from caring for, at that time, my two brothers and me, was a strong incentive that encouraged me to devote my personal and professional life reading, writing and teaching for the past 43 years. We were conspiring readers—she in the living room downstairs or in her bedroom, I under covers in my room, shared with my two brothers—but now blessedly empty and silent. I think it was the silent time and the excitement of entering the fictional worlds of the words that most attracted me.

I had a strategy for ritualizing this day or, if fortunate, days, off, especially if it was in the middle of winter snowstorms blowing across from Canada to the shores of Lake Erie only a half mile away: I would pile up blankets, build a fort under the covers, pull in my little cream-covered plastic radio, retrieve my flashlight from under the bed, pile 3 or 4 of the books next to me, and read. Nat King Cole, the Lennon Sisters or Big Band music from the Dorsey brothers or Les Brown "and his band of renown" would join me to provide gentle background music to my musings. I was, in those moments, perfectly happy and content in the cocoon of my ten year old life.

I recall as well that I loved horse stories and river stories and relished the X-Bar-X Brothers series or the Walter Farley series of adventures on horseback. Most gripping were the tales of Black Beauty, an Arabian stallion whose mythic hold on me has never loosened. I would then descend into the imaginative realm of narratives and linger with these lush geographies and adventures through the day, or at least until my mother would check with me to see if I felt could "keep down" a Canada Dry Ginger Ale or a bowl of Campbell's chicken noodle soup. Famished, I would muffle an affirmative so that in a short time lunch was served. The degree to which I sounded sick and remained so, to that extent I could squeeze at least two days of truancy in order to keep reading. My education took place with the good Ursuline Order of Sisters at Holy Cross Elementary School; but my learning happened under cover of illness with music and words weaving themselves together into a quilt of quiet days rich in narrative nesting. I believe that in these cold winter sojourns my love of solitude took root and deepened in the soil of my soul up to the present day.

In this way, along the corridor of feigning illness, my love of reading began and I sense, my love of learning in solitude wherein exploration overtook memorization and imagination trumped the competitive spirit of classroom decathlons. Looking back at these early memories and tracking them forward through high school and college and into teaching, I believe I was already sensing something hidden in the stories, something operating behind the curtain of math, geometry, philosophy, psychology, history, art and politics, some unknown specter, perhaps, that beckoned, like a magnetic attraction and I, only a shard of detritic steel, was inexorably borne toward it. What I realize now many years later was that I felt an affinity and a fascination with the mystery of things, perhaps of life itself, and that by pursuing it through as many reading runnels of understanding as possible, I might reach some contact with the nucleus of the numinous embedded in all things profane, each incubating its mysterious presence in the form of things.

I also found that I loved serving Mass as an altar boy at Holy Cross Catholic Church adjacent to my elementary school. Something about the sound of the Latin language held a mystery for me as I recited it by heart in the sanctuary where the miracle of the Mass was deployed. I liked as well the ritual uniform we put on to attend to the priest—we were called servers or altar boys—who had the power to consecrate unleavened wafers and altar wine into the body and blood of Christ, not in a ritual act of remembrance, we were admonished to distinguish, but as an act that conjured into presence God's Son in the moment. This intersection of the cross wherein time and eternity coalesced in the magic of the ritual fueled my imagination as it confused my sense of what was truly real.

These early experiences forged in me an interest in learning, never mind through what archway or series of metaphors; the shared values, however, were in reading, writing and speaking. The mystery and power of language itself to convey realities independent of and beyond the scope of my narrow world of experiences, to enliven and quicken my imagination to envision and at least grasp tentatively the problems inherent in different clusters of study, filled my existence with insights into the hidden and invisible realities of the world I could experience through the senses. I believe the love of humanities learning was inseminated in these early attractions for all things unknown.

Theorizing on conundrums, I was to learn later, was a way of imagining mythically; looking back now, I sense the study of myth was what I had been gravitating towards my entire life or at least a form of mythic consciousness that was at base poetic and symbolic. I was prodded along by some extraordinary teachers in high school as well as nurtured by several Ursuline Sisters in elementary school. At one point at St. Joseph's High School, a young Marianist brother by the name of William Pilder, my homeroom teacher during my sophomore year, gave me permission to take a novel from a long line of them that he brought to the classroom and lined up uniformly along the ledge that traversed the side windows of the room. These were his own books. I remember the title of one that contained the painting of an airplane on it that particularly drew my attention to it in the spring of 1961, some 50 years ago. It was entitled *Night Flight* by Antoine de Saint Exupéry. I was drawn to the title's dark voyage and asked Brother Pilder if I could borrow it. He immediately said, "Yes, but you may find it difficult." That was all he had to say. I took it home and devoured it one page at a time, determined to grasp its every nuance. It was a special book, exhilarating to read because he had believed I could read it, however haltingly. I returned it to him two weeks later and, pleased, he invited me to borrow others that attracted me. From him I learned a core lesson on the art of teaching and mentoring: open opportunities for students to pass through. Then get out of their way.

The attraction to literature grew in part because of my ripening but still vague awareness that the stories dealt with dilemmas and conflicts that implicated philosophy, theology, politics, history, psychology and economics. Often, human dilemmas were not clearly drawn nor were their conclusions neat and safely packaged; but the process in the prose was delicious and allowed or forced me as a reader to read with several pairs of eyes at the same time. Poets, I soon discovered, were not interested in answers, be they facile or difficult; rather, their interest was in rendering a human dilemma in multiple terms and to offer often paradoxical returns for the reader's efforts. I sensed that these fields of poetry, myth and psychology were hugely satisfying in their study of what William Faulkner called "the human heart in conflict with itself" (Noble Prize Acceptance Speech, 119) and writing about these areas of knowing both challenging and gratifying. Literature revealed how "Homo homini lupus," which Freud, quoting Plautus, translated as "Man is a wolf to man" (*Civilization* 69). I hungered to know the origins of suffering and redemption, having lived within constant anguish in an unsettled household for most of my younger years.

At the same time I intuitively recoiled from specializing in an area of study, struggling rather to keep my education broadly-based and generally-ranged. I guess, then, that I have adhered to and sought continually to faithfully renew my membership in the Club for Dilettantes. Often given a bad name, the word *dilettante* I use in the spirit in which Henrich Zimmer casts it in *The King and the Corpse*. In his chapter entitled "The Dilettante Among Symbols," he relates how the word means "to take delight in" (2). He then goes on to suggest that "the moment we abandon this dilettante attitude toward the images of folklore and myth and begin to feel certain about their proper interpretation . . . we deprive ourselves of the quickening contact, the demonic and inspiring assault that is the effect of their intrinsic virtue" (2).

What brought me to the underpinnings of what was developing into an eclectic learning style firmly riveted in the humanities, and from there stretching towards any source that galvanized my interest, was an event that occurred when I was twenty years old; it was comprised of such force that it reset the compass for the rest of my life. The short version goes like this:

At age 20 I was a deputy bailiff in a Municipal Court in Euclid, Ohio. At the same time, I attended a community college in downtown Cleveland two nights a week, majoring in Sociology. I had just bought a new car, was dating a young woman I liked very much and was bored out of my well-ironed shirt. In one of the courses I enrolled in for fall semester night school was another bored bloke, Dennis Collins, who wrote a weekly sports column for *The Cleveland Press*. After class we quickly cultivated the habit of drifting over to a pub in downtown Cleveland and sharing our feelings of growing restlessness. One evening, after class, we were compelled by some hazy but stubborn desire to explore the offices of the Cleveland docks, a busy port which saw ships from all over the world sail down the St. Lawrence Seaway into the Great Lakes region to unload and pick up cargo. We met quite by chance a man, head of the shipping traffic, and asked about booking passage on a ship to Europe. He told us that, given developing circumstances on a German freighter that was due in the Cleveland port in two weeks, if we wished to work our passage, he had two crew positions open when the ship arrived from Detroit on its way back to its home port in Bremerhaven, Germany. If we wanted to work passage, we had to be at the dock two weeks from this very night, passports in hand and duffel bags filled and at the ready. It was as if we both awoke at that moment from a sluggish dream courtesy of a cold bucket of Lake Erie water.

We made the arrangements and sailed on June 5, 1966 on a route up the St. Lawrence Seaway and across the Atlantic Ocean to Bremerhaven, a trip that was to last three weeks. Ten of those days we were out of sight of any land as we sailed high into the North Atlantic before dropping down into one of the largest European ports in the region. We then hitchhiked our way to southern Ireland and stayed with relatives neither of us had ever met. Vietnam and the draft, however, breathed its fire down our necks in Ireland, forcing us to fly home with great dispatch from Shannon Airport.

Those weeks on the ship comprised a passage into another reality; every night I sat aft with the seagulls that joined us for the voyage, flying during the day as they dove for food remnants thrown overboard after the crew had eaten, then roosting on the railings at night. There in the private company of a dozen white gulls, I faithfully wrote in my journal of that day's adventures. Dennis and I were the only two non-Germans on board. The crew consisted of merchant seamen satisfying their two year military obligation in Germany. Some were fiercely anti-American, including the captain, so we learned quickly to stay out of their brooding way. I discovered something elemental changing in me as a result of this time on the ocean *and* in the act of writing in my first journal.

When I returned home, I typed up the manuscript and found I had written over 150 pages. I also began, just as importantly, devouring every tale of the sea I could lay hands on: Richard Henry Dana's *Two Years Before the Mast*, Joseph Conrad's sea tales, Herman Melville's *White Jacket* and *Billy Budd* and then the BIG leviathanic narrative, *Moby-Dick*. I still remember thinking at the time: If these writers can capture so much of what I felt, thought, imagined, suffered on this voyage, then this kind of writing is worthy of study. I changed my major that fall from psychology to literature in the English Department of the newly-formed Cleveland State University.

What I had come to was a container of sorts that held my imagination tight to itself: the power of analogy and the integrating grace of metaphor. These two qualities or acts of the imagination, however, did not necessarily need to spring from stories alone; they might find their way into my soul through theory, philosophy, psychology, theology, spiritual writings as well as my own travel writings. What I became certain of was that there existed something essential about the way these disciplines related to one another and could be studied within an imaginal container of mirrors, each refracting off one another to reveal what the others did not. I found it was like studying a mosaic close up, with each set of stones offering a partial image of the whole; when one then stepped back, something marvelous and miraculous fell into focus, allowing one to discern the contours of the entire image or idea that could lead to a larger reality whose allusiveness might remain constant if seen through only one discipline. I also discovered the joy that attended insights one could claim as one's own, built stone by stone in part, by the mosaic understandings of others throughout history. I had seen, however briefly, the large tradition of learning through the apertures of individual works.

This joy, this feeling of aliveness at being present at the birth of an idea, was full of gut excitement. There was as well an accompanying feeling of frustration and expenditure of enormous energy when I attempted to write this insight into such a form that others might find interesting, attractive, or even be persuaded by its validity and worth. Writing is part of the humanities learning schema that, in pulling from the lexicons of so many disciplines, can assist one to ward off the empty jargon of one field or specialization, that can trap one into simply mimicking the expression of others. But to work from a humanities-based vocabulary allows one to experiment with new metaphors because one's "word horde" is greater, more varied and diverse, less susceptible to rigid formats or phrases suffering exhaustion from overuse.

The imagination seems to thrive on being elastic, flexible, supple, nuanced, darkening at times, lightening up at others; it also seems to relish dialogue with other fields of knowing, pulling from this one, challenging that one, offering a new combination of two others, seeking originality in the commonplace, even the sacred in what seems so normative and already digested. Always at work is the soul's subtle movement—cyclic, circuitous, slippery, sharply focused—but not dogmatically obsessive with the idea that one has found the only answer worth adopting. The subtle range of its options increases to the extent one is familiar and conversant with other modes of knowing. Epistemology needs several wardrobes, ample variety of fashions, an abundant but not excessive wardrobe to play the roles it is asked to don through multiple disciplines.

I discovered in this slow pilgrimage to the inside of various structures of knowing a mythic sensibility, a way of thinking along mythic corridors that is immensely facilitated through humanities-leaning learning. Watch the work of Marie Louise von Franz, C.G. Jung, Joseph Campbell, Marion Woodman, James Hillman, Sigmund Freud, Gaston Bachelard, Fyodor Dostoevsky, and much earlier in history Homer, Plotinus, Plato, Aristotle, Sophocles, Aeschylus, Virgil, and one may discern how many disciplines they exploit to deploy new ideas, not old ones repackaged but finally insubstantial in their construction.

The qualities as well as actions of invocation and evocation appeared to grow organically from the analogical bent of the imagination to see the pattern, to discern the underlying principles governing a thing or assembling an idea, to remember the connection from earlier sources, to retain the qualities of *then* to pull them into *now,* the energic reality of form beneath phenomenal structures, to spiral back into history and across disciplines and return to where one was in contemplation in order to renovate an old pattern to a new purpose. The power of knowing the tradition in several disciplines gives the human imagination a range of motion that an arthritic grinding bone on bone prohibits. This range of motion and emotion is one of the strongest attributes in allowing a mythic sensibility to gestate and grow in the soul.

I have thought for some time that any presidential cabinet should include not only a humanities learner but also a mythologist in the room when the big decisions are being contemplated because these sources might offer a cultural and multifaceted depiction of a country and its people. In each discipline of learning lurks a nuclear reactor, a unique energy field that is activated when we step into it. It is revved up even more when we enter donning the suit of another discipline so that some nuclear core reverberation may be set in motion because of just such a confrontation/conversation.

In his essay that introduces Sigmund Freud's *Civilization and its*

Discontents, the biographer Peter Gay opens with the opinion that "it was Freud's fate, as he observed not without pride, to 'agitate the sleep of mankind'" (ix). I like this idea of agitating the sleepers, those needing a bit of prodding towards consciousness. The humanities behave as a constellation of consciousness-altering disciplines; when taken together, they can evoke and provoke one into a fuller awareness, to see below the phenomenal world into those principles and patterns that give them their structure and form. Absent the humanities, this slumber will continue in the modern mind to darken the possibility of an informed and thoughtful collective that has been evaporating on the horizon of culture for decades.

REFERENCES

Darwin, Charles. 1876/2004. *The Origin of Species*. Edison, NJ: Castle Books.

Faulkner, William. 1965. "Address Upon Receiving the Noble Prize for Literature." Stockholm, December 10, 1950. *Essays, Speeches & Public Letters*. Ed. James Meriwether. New York: Random House. 119-120.

Freud, Sigmund. 1961. *Civilization and Its Discontents*. The Standard Edition. Introduction Peter Gay. Trans. James Strachey. New York: Norton.

Zimmer, Heinrich. 1993. *The King and the Corpse*. Ed. Joseph Campbell. Bollingen Series XI. Princeton: Princeton UP.

100+ INFLUENTIAL BOOKS

For the moment excluding music, paintings, sculptures, architectural structures that have shaped me as well, I hone in on books that have influenced my thought at various junctures of my development. While the overwhelming majority of them are literary titles, they nonetheless provoke in the soul so many of the disciplines comprising the humanities that they might best be understood as containers for humanities conversations.

- Fyodor Dostoevsky, *Crime and Punishment*
- Fyodor Dostoevsky, *The Idiot*
- Fyodor Dostoevsky, *The Brothers Karamazov*
- James Joyce, *Dubliners*
- James Joyce, *A Portrait of the Artist as a Young Man*
- Flannery O'Connor, *Complete Short Stories*

- Herman Hesse, *Siddhartha*
- Herman Hesse, *The Glass Bead Game*
- James Hillman, *Revisioning Psychology*
- James Hillman, *The Myth of Analysis*
- Maurice Merleau-Ponty, *The Phenomenology of Perception*
- Maurice Merleau-Ponty, *The Primacy of Perception: And   Other Essays on Phenomenological Psychology*
- Joseph Campbell, *The Power of Myth*
- Joseph Campbell, *The Inner Reaches of Outer Space*
- Joseph Campbell, *The Hero with a Thousand Faces*
- Carl Gustav Jung, *Archetypes and the Collective Unconscious*
- Carl Gustav Jung, *Aion, Researches into the Phenomenology of the Self*
- Carl Gustav Jung, *Civilization in Transition*
- Carl Gustav Jung, *Modern Man in Search of a Soul*
- Carl Gustav Jung, *Memories, Dreams, Reflections*
- Homer*: The Iliad*
- Homer, *The Odyssey*
- Dante Alighieri, *The Divine Comedy*
- William Faulkner, *As I Lay Dying*
- William Faulkner, *Light in August*
- Thomas Mann, *Death in Venice and other Short Stories*
- Shirley Jackson, "The Lottery"
- James Baldwin, *The Fire Next Time*
- James Baldwin, *Go Tell It on the Mountain*
- Eudora Welty, *Complete Short Stories*
- John Milton, *Paradise Lost*
- Thomas Moore, *Care of the Soul*
- Thomas Merton, *Conjectures of a Guilty Bystander*
- Thomas Merton, *Seeds/New Seeds of Contemplation*
- *Upanishads*
- Plotinus, *Enneads*
- Evelyn Underwood, *Mysticism*
- Robert Romanyshyn, *Technology as Symptom and Dream*
- Donald Cowan, *Unbinding Prometheus: Education for the Coming Age*
- Jacques Barzun, *The House of Intellect*
- Jacques Barzun, *The Art of Teaching*
- The Essays of Louise Cowan on Poetry and Poetic Knowledge
- Louise Cowan*: Literary Genres* (in various places)
- T.S. Eliot, *Complete Poems and Plays*

- Francis Yates, *The Art of Memory*
- Eugene Minkowski, *Lived Time*
- Herman Melville, *Moby-Dick*
- Herman Melville, *Billy Budd*
- Toni Morrison, *Beloved*
- Ralph Waldo Emerson, *Essays*
- H. D. Thoreau, *Walden*
- Sigmund Freud, *The Interpretation of Dreams*
- Thich Nhat Hanh, *Thich Nhat Hanh Collection*
- Northrop Frye: *The Anatomy of Criticism*
- Russell Lockhart, *Words as Eggs*
- Aristotle, *Poetics*
- Plato: *Dialogues*
- *The Epic of Gilgamesh*
- *The Old and New Testaments*
- Oscar Wilde, *The Picture of Dorian Gray*
- J.D. Salinger, *The Catcher in the Rye*
- Jack Miles, *God: A Biography*
- Shakespeare, *Othello, King Lear, Macbeth, Hamlet, A Midsummer Night's Dream, The Merchant of Venice, All's Well that Ends Well*
- Sophocles, *The Theban Trilogy*
- Euripides, *The Bacchae*
- Ayn Rand, *Atlas Shrugged*
- Ayn Rand, *The Fountainhead*
- Jean Jacques Rousseau, *Confessions*
- Wole Soyinka, *Death and the King's Horseman*
- Margaret Edson, *Wit*
- John Milton, *Paradise Lost*
- Wallace Stevens, *The Complete Poems and Essays*
- Bruno Barnhart, *Second Simplicity: The Inner Life of Christianity*
- Owen Barfield, *Saving the Appearances*
- Vaclav Havel, *The Art of the Impossible*
- José Ortega y Gasset, *Meditations on Quijote*
- Leo Tolstoy, *The Death of Ivan Ilych*
- Leo Tolstoy, *Anna Karenina*
- Richard Selzer, *Confessions of a Knife*
- Richard Selzer, *Mortal Lessons*
- Edmund Husserl, *The Crisis of European Sciences and Transcendental Phenomenology*

- Elie Wiesel, *Night*
- Primo Levi, *Survival in Auschwitz*
- John Keats, *Selected Letters and Poems*
- Hannah Arendt, *Men in Dark Times*
- Rupert Sheldrake, *The Presence of the Past*
- Giambatisto Vico, *The New Science*
- Meister Eckhart, *Complete Works*
- Denis Donoghue, *The Practice of Reading*
- Richard Weaver, *Visions of Order*
- Jacques Le Groff, *History and Memory*
- Eric Auerbach, *Mimesis: Representations of Reality in Western Literature*
- Wendell Berry, *The Unsettling of America: Culture and Agriculture*
- Annie Dillard, *Pilgrim at Tinker Creek*
- Gaston Bachelard, *The Poetics of Space*
- Gaston Bachelard, *Earth and Reveries of Will*
- Gaston Bachelard, *On Poetic Imagination and Reverie*
- Louise Rosenblatt, *The Reader, the Text, the Poem*
- Mircea Eliade, *The Myth of the Eternal Return*
- Mircea Eliade, *The Sacred and the Profane*
- St. Augustine, *The Confessions*
- Aeschylus, *The Oresteis*
- Albert Camus, *The Plague*
- Albert Camus, *The Myth of Sisyphus and Other Essays*
- William V. Spanov, *Existentialism: A Casebook*
- Graham Green, *The Power and the Glory*
- Jean Paul Sartre, *No Exit*
- Rollo May, *Love and Will*
- Rollo May, *Power and Innocence*
- Rollo May, *A Casebook on Existential Psychology and Psychiatry*
- Morris Berman, *Coming to Our Senses: Body and Spirit in the Hidden History of the West*
- Gerald May, *Addiction and Grace*
- Eudora Welty, *One Writer's Beginning*
- Dennis Patrick Slattery, *Harvesting Darkness: Essays on Literature, Myth, Film and Culture*
- Dennis Patrick Slattery, *A Limbo of Shards: Essays on Memory, Myth and Metaphor*
- Dennis Patrick Slattery, *Grace in the Desert: Awakening to the Gifts of Monastic Life*

- Alexander Solzynitshn, *One Day in the Life of Ivan Denisovich*
- Jacques Maritain, *Creative Intuition in Art and Poetry*
- Max Picard, *The World of Silence*

THE REPOSITORY OF HUMAN WISDOM

Though written in different voices from different positions, the essayists in this section all make the same point: the path to wisdom lies in doing away with either/or thinking about the dichotomy between the STEM disciplines (science, technology, engineering, and math) and the disciplines under the umbrella of the humanities, and embracing both. Michael Sipiora takes natural science to task for its dismissal of the human sciences, the latter with its affinity to the humanities. He writes, "insofar as the humanities deal with meanings as well as facts, they are granted no validity from the perspective of natural sciences because only facts, never meanings, can be experimentally validated." From his position as a psychologist and an educator, he argues that psychology conceived of and taught only as a natural science is thoughtless and soulless, reducing us to the status of "an information-processing machine." Yet, he doesn't argue that psychology should do away with the gifts of the natural sciences. Instead, he writes, "I know that while many things about human beings can be explained in the same experiential manner that took us to the moon and produced the nuclear bomb, the most significant things, from my perspective, are the things about human beings that elude quantification and are therefore unavailable to explanation by way of experimentation. It is this qualitative dimension of human being that is brought into view by the humanities."

My essay takes up the themes of both the moon race and the nuclear bomb as I trace the tensions between technology and the humanities in American education, and the politics and economics that drive a wedge between the two. Hitching my metaphorical star on the mythological twins Castor and Pollux, I argue for the importance of a twinned education combining both technology and the humanities. It didn't occur to me until after I wrote the essay that combining technology and the humanities is exactly what I do in my work at Pacifica Graduate Institute as Academic Chair of Hybrid Programs. Hybrid education combines the best of face-to-face learning with a technological component of online learning, and here, especially in our master's degree in Engaged Humanities and the Creative Life, we've found a way to combine technology and the humanities in very meaningful ways.

Gwyn Wood is the Senior Admissions counselor for that same degree program, which is also apropos given that she was raised under the influence of the humanities with the tutelage of her English professor father and her librarian mother. Thinking she had learned everything she could from the humanities, she set off to study the sciences in college, only to learn that there was no fundamental distinction between the two; they simply use different language to explore the same "big questions" of life. Where Sipiora and Selig make serious arguments against the pitting and privileging of one distinct discipline over another, Wood takes a different tact and shows how arbitrary such distinctions can be, lifting herself above the fray and showing us how the whole of education is an enterprise which "ask[s] eternal questions that relate to our understanding of ourselves as a species, our purpose in life and our relationship with the world we live in."

Jennifer Leigh Selig

And yet we face monumental challenges that have not, nor will they, give way to only quantitative, instrumental responses—from the violence and addictions that rock our communities, to the climate crisis, to the wars of territory and terror that circle the globe, to the threatened collapse of financial structures and the ever-widening disparities of wealth. Ironically, what we now desperately need is the understanding afforded by the human sciences, a qualitative sense-making informed by the insights and vision of the humanities.

~Michael P. Sipiora

The humanities are the limbs of education that grow the soul, express the spirit, and contain the repository of human wisdom, the storehouse of our grand experiment in social living, offering a place to discuss the ends for which we live. In the humanities reside the big questions—what makes life worth living? What values should shape the life of the individual and the life of the nation?—and in the humanities we learn the critical thinking tools we need to engage the questions and begin to discern, articulate, and apply our answers. Technology may be the two legs we stand upon, but the humanities are our two arms, able to reach out and transform a neighborhood into a brotherhood.

~**Jennifer Leigh Selig**

Throughout my first term of college I realized the lessons I had learned from novels, from history, and from art were all present in the chemistry lectures I attended and the physics labs I slaved over. . . . The professors told me matter was finite, change occurred and the universe demanded balance. This was the same lecture I had heard when studying Hinduism—some of the vocabulary just happened to be different. Exchange the term "reactant" for that of "prakiti" (matter, creative energy) and the idea was the same. The larger "truth" that lay beneath an exquisitely balanced chemical equation was the same piece of knowledge that a careful reading of the "Mahabharata" could yield.

~**Gwyn Wood**

PSYCHOLOGY IS UNTHINKABLE WITHOUT THE HUMANITIES

Michael P. Sipiora, Ph.D.

PREFACE

In what follows I will be discussing psychology exclusively, but the situation I decry and the dilemma I critique are not unique to that field. All of the "human sciences"—history, sociology, theology, and anthropology, along with psychology—currently face an existential challenge. The human sciences are rigorous and systematic in their understandings of human affairs, but they are not driven by the experimental method of the natural sciences (Giorgi 1970). Contrary to the natural sciences' rejection of the subjectivism of the humanities, the human sciences affirm and are enhanced by their historical and theoretical affinities with the humanities. Because of these and other differences from the natural science model, the continuation of the human sciences as reputable and reliable kinds of knowledge is being called into question.

The present cultural milieu, under the sway of technological intoxication and calculative blindness, has been arrogantly dismissive of the human sciences. It has initiated an inquisition in which these disciplines either deny any affiliation with the humanities and adopt the approach of the natural sciences or suffer a funding death. College courses, even whole departments, decline as fewer and fewer students can afford to pursue a humanities or human science degree. Qualitative human science research remains unsupported as grant funding comes with requirements for empirical, quantitative foundations for all projects.

Without cultural acknowledgement and support, the human sciences are in danger of being "disappeared" by an ever-increasing demand for natural science validity and reliability in all affairs even those distinctively human matters that call for qualitative understanding. And yet we face monumental challenges that have not, nor will they, give way to only quantitative, instrumental responses—from the violence and addictions that rock our communities, to the climate crisis, to the wars of territory and terror that circle the globe, to the threatened collapse of financial structures and the ever-widening disparities of wealth. Ironically, what we now desperately need is the understanding afforded by the human sciences, a qualitative sense-making informed by the insights and vision of the humanities. While acknowledging the powerful and continuing need for ever more advanced calculation, what we risk losing with the devaluing of the humanities and the decline of the human sciences, and yet what we most need, is imagination.

INTRODUCTION

I am writing as a psychologist whose career has been in both doctoral level education and in the practice of psychotherapy. As a university professor, I helped educate students in a humanities-based understanding of psychology—a theoretically sophisticated education that was superordinate to their clinical training. Unfortunately such an education, and the clinical practices based upon it, is under attack. Demands for competency-driven training, instruction in the most up-to-date natural science information, and a focus on empirically-based clinical practice collude with psychology's professionalism and its (unintended, yet nevertheless unholy) alliance with a repressive status quo.

In my work as a psychotherapist, I have come to believe that the suffering brought into the therapy room is less the product of individual deficiencies or deficits and more the production of life in a world increasingly inhospitable to human dwelling. The lack of community, tradition, and shared meaning (Cushman 1990), economic pressures and the degradation of the environment, global chaos and political meltdown, along with the dizzying and disintegrating effects of technological "progress," make it harder and harder to live a genuinely human life—however one may define it. This results in the kinds of distress—the anxiety, depression, addictions, behavioral problems—for which people seek psychological treatment. In providing such treatment there arises the danger of foisting problems, whose origins are essentially social and political in character, on to the backs of individuals by blaming faulty upbringing or congenital failures. There is also the danger of conspiring in the perpetuation and reinforcement of the very conditions that have provoked individual distress. To avoid these dangers and begin to contemplate an appropriate response requires that we rethink the way we imagine the world and ourselves in it, and that, as I see it, is a matter of the humanities. Without such attention to the humanities, psychotherapists mistake their calling and fall prey to agendas in their professional practice that they would not consciously affirm nor intentionally carry out (Cushman 1990).

Within this context, I intend to reflect on how the title of my essay—"psychology is unthinkable without the humanities"—is true in several senses. First, for me as a teacher and therapist, it is unthinkable—inconceivable—that I would have or even *could* have become a psychologist without the path opened by the humanities. What I learned from the humanities led me to psychology. Second, my conception of psychology, as one can easily surmise, is utterly and completely informed by the humanities, particularly philosophy and literature. This thoughtfulness is a hallmark of depth psychologies—psychoanalytical, analytical, phenomenological—exemplified in sophisticated conceptions of psychological life as a reality of reflection lived in and through the cultural world. Third, psychology is fundamentally unthinkable, in the sense of being thoughtless or ill-conceived, without the humanities. Psychology conceived only as empirical, positivistic natural science fails to provide an adequate conception of psychological life. On this point it is important to note that I am not contending that psychology should be conceived without the benefit of the natural sciences. Rather, the point is that the conceptualization of psychology requires both the humanities and the natural sciences.

I. THE HUMANITIES LED ME TO PSYCHOLOGY

I was fortunate to have attended a progressive, liberal arts-oriented high school in the San Francisco Bay Area in the early 1970s. What was on everyone's mind (besides sex, drugs, and rock & roll) was how to change the world. Classes with titles such as "Love as a Concept" and "The Hero in Science Fiction" were the fare of the day; philosophy, literature, and the study of world cultures made an impression on me. I still remember listening to my academic councilor (who himself was in graduate school studying psychology) explain existentialism.

Concerned about the political situation in the United States—Vietnam, poverty, discrimination, to name a few—I had started college at West Valley Community College as a pre-law, history major. The idea was to go to law school as a route to political activity that would bring about change. Then, in a philosophy of law class (at San Jose State University), I read classicist Norman O. Brown's inspired, mind-blowing response to the politics of the 1960s: *Love's Body*. It was all about changing the world by changing the way we imagine reality. In order to even try to begin to understand *Love's Body* I had to read Brown's earlier *Life Against Death: The Psychoanalytical Meaning of History,* which in turn necessitated that I read Sigmund Freud and encounter his radical notions of repression and the unconscious.

Brown's erudite interpretation of Freud and his critique of the repressive dynamics of modern civilization led me to take-up philosophy. (I didn't find much interest in these ideas in the psychology department). I was extremely lucky to study philosophy with exceptional professors. They were respected scholars who were also incredible teachers. They were classically educated and culturally sophisticated. They wrote on art, psychology, and, even business. Their existential, phenomenological orientation, with its sense of wonder and appreciation of human finitude, captured my imagination and inspired further study. I spent longer in philosophy than I had intended so that law school was put aside for a Master's degree in that discipline.

My academic goals had changed from a desire to go to law school as a path into politics, to the study of philosophy as a foundation for understanding the political realm. In the course of these changes I read Karl Marx and took to heart his insistence that while philosophers have interpreted the world, the real point is to change it. I decide to pursue graduate studies in psychology because I felt that psychology had a direct involvement with the meanings in people's lives and that changing the world necessarily involved working with these meanings. By this time I had also encountered Martin Heidegger's contention that technology reduces everything to a resource, including human beings, as well as his critique of merely calculative, instrumental thinking. I knew that understanding meaning requires another kind of thinking—imagination or a meditative kind of thinking—and that such understanding exceeded the causal explanations of contemporary natural scientific psychology. But I had to search out a psychology program that actually thought about things in this way.

Hardly the conventional natural psychology program, my doctoral studies in phenomenological and archetypal psychology (at the University of Dallas), required minors in both literature and interdisciplinary studies. Like my teachers in philosophy, my psychology professors were scholars educated in the humanities; in addition, they were also practicing psychotherapists. They turned my attention to imagination as a non-technological disclosure of reality that accessed meaning and symbol, to history and culture as the context and horizons of our shared existence and to the metaphorical character of psychological life as portrayed in the Western literary tradition. My dissertation addressed the alienation of psychological life occurring in our technological culture that announces itself in the distress people present in psychotherapy. Modeled on classical rhetoric and informed by a Heideggerian understanding of humans, world, and technology, this response was meant to be a cultural therapeutic that spoke to the contemporary plight of human dwelling.

For the next twenty-plus years I taught in a clinical psychology department (at Duquesne University) that is accredited by the American Psychological Association and for over six decades has been a center for a human science alternative to the conventional, natural science-based approaches to the discipline. I taught psychology as a human science which seeks to understand, by way of qualitative description and interpretation, the meanings inherent in people's experience. I taught philosophically and literarily sophisticated approaches to social psychology, psychotherapy, and research. And I followed one of my teachers, James Hillman, in teaching depth psychology as part of a tradition reaching back beyond Freud and Carl Jung to the Romantic poets and Neoplatonic philosophers.

I am now a core faculty member in an institution devoted to depth psychology (Pacifica Graduate Institute) and a licensed clinical psychologist because that is where I was led by an education in the humanities. The project of contributing to a more just world—inspired, informed, and transformed by the ideas and art of the humanities—abides in the education I offer students and in my own clinical practice. A humanities education has made me ever vigilant of the danger of "helping" clients employ coping strategies and behavior modifications in the service of chasing happiness through efficient work and satisfying consumption. In place of the monstrous computer model that dominates contemporary psychology (mind is software, brain is hardware; psychological distress is to be addressed by cognitive restructuring to correct faulty "software" and pharmacological interventions to correct chemical imbalances in the "hardware"), I turn to the humanities and its way of imagining the acting and suffering person.

At this point we have the other two senses, introduced above, in which I take psychology to be unthinkable without the humanities. The computer model of human beings illustrates my third sense insofar as it takes itself as a calculative construction of "objective" facts and eschews the ideas and images of the humanities. On the other hand, the notion of "acting and suffering" as "constitut[ing] the very fabric of a life," quoting philosopher Paul Ricoeur (1991, 28), exemplifies the thoughtfulness that the humanities bring to psychology. It is to this second sense in which psychology is unthinkable without the humanities that I next turn.

II. MY UNDERSTANDING OF PSYCHOLOGY ORIGINATES IN THE HUMANITIES

Because my path to psychology was paved by the humanities, it makes sense that my understanding of psychology reflects the humanities in imagining the human being in the context of and in dialogue with the history of Western culture. But while there are particular and personal reasons for my way of understanding psychology, there is also—and more importantly—a persuasive, philosophical reason. Psychology, as does every scientific discipline, presupposes an understanding of the "human being" and of the nature of "reality." Which is to say that there is an implicit philosophical anthropology—as in *anthropos*, the Greek term for "human being"—and a metaphysics, a philosophical understanding of reality, in psychological science. Accordingly, a discipline's foundation is a philosophical matter that precedes, rather than is based upon, science.

The understanding of psychology as a human science, noted above, follows upon the nineteenth century German philosopher Wilhelm Dilthey's distinction between two kinds of science: natural science which explains reality in terms of measurable, experimentally explained causal relationships, and human science which attempts to understand the meaningful reality of being human in qualitative terms (Giorgi 1970). Human scientific psychology, such as the existential psychology of Rollo May, has an explicit and critically examined philosophical foundation and is in dialogue with the understandings of human being presented in the arts and literature. For example, May approvingly references the observation of his teacher, the theologian and philosopher Paul Tillich:

> Picasso's painting *Guernica* gives the most gripping and revealing portrait of the atomistic, fragmentized condition of European society that precedes World War II and "shows what is now in the souls of many Americans as disruptiveness, existential doubt, emptiness, and meaninglessness." (1958, 17)

Conventional natural scientific psychology also has a philosophical foundation: the real is what is measurable, quantifiable, and factual. This philosophical worldview, first articulated clearly and distinctly by Descartes, provided the foundation for all the modern disciplines that arose in the Scientific Revolution from the queen of these new sciences—physics—to the last of the disciplines to establish itself on a factual, experimental basis—psychology. Contemporary natural scientific psychology's computer model of the human being, to which I earlier referred, is an outgrowth of this view of reality and also the heir to Descartes' mechanistic conception of the body. I will come back to these points in the next section, but here it is important to note that insofar as the humanities deal with meanings as well as facts, they are granted no validity from the perspective of natural sciences because only facts, never meanings, can be experimentally validated.

So my dilemma must be immediately clear. I had turned to psychology because I wished to gain access to and understand the meanings in people's lives. Natural scientific psychology would tell me that such meanings are merely subjective, not objective facts, and that they are produced by causal factors that call for operational definition and experiential investigation. But I have seen prints of Picasso's *Guernica* and so I know better. I know that while many things about human beings can be explained in the same experiential manner that took us to the moon and produced the nuclear bomb (Romanyshyn 1989), the most significant things, from my perspective, are the things about human beings that elude quantification and are therefore unavailable to explanation by way of experimentation. It is this qualitative dimension of human being that is brought into view by the humanities.

The question now becomes not whether psychology should be based in philosophy but rather which philosophy could be the basis for a psychology adequate to grasping meaning? Which view of reality and the human being allows us access to qualitative phenomena and thereby to meaning? To this question there is no one answer. There are numerous philosophies that offer approaches for human science psychology from Heidegger's phenomenology as the foundation for existential psychology to the Neoplatonism that orients Hillman's version of depth psychology, archetypal psychology. And in these two cases, existential psychology and archetypal psychology, it is not only philosophy but the humanities in general, as I noted above, that inform their perspectives as human science psychologies. What the philosophical approaches that provide a foundation for human science psychologies have in common is that they all recognize that the human capacity to make sense of things, what can be broadly and inclusively conceived of as "reason," cannot be limited to the calculative or instrumental rationality that is the hallmark of the modern natural sciences. In addition to calculative rationality, there is the disclosure of meaning by way of qualitative understanding. May cited "ecstatic reason" (1958). Hillman referred to "imagination" (1975). Heidegger discussed "meditative thinking" (quoted in Sipiora 1991). No matter its name, this kind of sense-making never denies the natural scientific calculation of facts but includes the creative, interpretative, and expansive understandings exemplified in the arts and literature, in music and drama, in the whole array of disciplines that comprise the humanities but have been disenfranchised from psychology when modeled on the natural sciences. It is this kind of sense-making that grasps the invisibles—the dimensions of being human that forever elude quantification—and allows us to comprehend meanings.

In my own work as a psychologist—both teacher and therapist—it is, as already mentioned, Ricoeur's vision of the human being offered in his philosophical studies of narrative, that I have found most powerful. Human beings as acting and suffering: interacting with others, things, and the world in general; being acted upon, undergoing the encounters with others and things, and the world in general. Ricoeur's work spanned the humanities: phenomenology and psychoanalysis, rhetoric and metaphor, evil and ethics, hermeneutics and theology. In identifying the quality, the "what-kind-ed-ness," of human being as "acting and suffering," we recognize that the "fabric of life" is woven of both fact and meaning. I necessarily include not just measurable facts but also the significance of acts and how they matter, the intelligibility of things we suffer. With the notion of acting and suffering, the natural scientific pretense to timeless universality dissipates and the socio-historical character of human being comes into view. Universality depends on facts that are independent of context; meaning is always a matter of context. Meaning, culturally constructed and historically configured, becomes the materiality of our psychological reality and we are figured not as information processing machines but as those who act and suffer within a storied life (Sipiora 2008). Such a life defies mere causal explanation and calls to be contemplated through ecstatic reason, imagination, and meditative thinking.

III. PSYCHOLOGY IS ILL-CONCEIVED WITHOUT THE HUMANITIES

As I have related above, every scientific discipline is conceived on the basis of a philosophical view of reality and human being. What makes conventional natural scientific psychology's conception monstrous is not that it is limited. All views are limited, and of course some are more so than others. The issue, as Romanyshyn (1989) has demonstrated both historically and philosophically, is that the natural scientific stance denies it is a conceptualization and instead blindly insists that it is a specification of what is, that it depicts reality as it is in and of itself. Thus the natural science view acknowledges no limits other than the extent of its own development while it judges all other ways of seeing to be inferior, defective, and incorrect. Anything qualitative in character has to be reduced to a measurable quantity, preferably by an operational definition. What is lost is the reality of the qualitative phenomenon with which the process began. What the process arrives at, especially when one is dealing with human being, is not that with which you started—which is both the point and the problem. Sorrow exceeds its explanation as an electrochemical process in the brain (Sipiora 2012b). Stress is more disguised than defined by calculations of demands and resources. The problem, again especially when concerned with the human, is that the very things that are left behind, so to speak, are the things that matter from the perspective of human beings who act and suffer. For all the benefit that operationally conceiving of human beings as advanced organic computers offers, its inability to even acknowledge the integrity of the qualitative dimensions of being human, nay its abject denial of the reality of these dimensions, leaves behind a human being without any humanity. Such a view is monstrous in that it offers a calculative definition of human being devoid of the qualities that have long defined the human condition in art, literature, music, history, and philosophy.

Psychology conceived as a natural science is definitely thoughtless, and is so by design: calculation trumps thinking. The calculations of experimental reason are the ultimate mode of sense-making pursued by such a psychology; its persistent goal is to purge itself of all other kinds of reason (ecstatic reason, imagination, meditative thinking). Calculation is the only valid, truthful kind of sense-making. Throughout his career James Hillman lamented the exclusionary literalisms, reductionist explanatory models, and the poverty of ideas that continually plagues natural science psychology. Heidegger (1968) observed that what is most thought-provoking today is that we do not think, that we are not provoked to think because we feel that there is no need. We hold fast to the idea that everything can be—if not now, then in the future—calculated, that is, quantitatively described, explained, predicted, and ultimately controlled. For Heidegger what is at risk in this absence of meditative thinking or lack of imagination is our very humanity. Without such thinking we are reduced to an information-processing machine.

Among the phenomena that are invariably left out, in the intentional thoughtlessness of scientific calculations, is what the humanities call the soul or the psyche—that for which it would seem the discipline of psychology was named. While a phantom or fabrication to be vanquished in modern natural science, the psyche has always held a place of the highest rank in the humanities. Psyche figures prominently in literature, art, and music and holds the attention of philosophy from ancient to postmodern. Hillman (1975) describes the psyche as that which makes meaning possible by transforming events, deepening them into experiences. Following the influence of Heidegger, existential psychologist Medard Boss (1988) understands the psyche in terms of the human being as a "world-spanning openness" in which things can appear, be immediately perceived, grasped and responded to in their inherent meaningfulness (Sipiora 2000). While differing in their philosophical orientation, both Hillman and Boss associate the psyche with the qualitative dimensions of human being that, from their respective perspectives, make us most human.

To conceive of psychology on the basis of calculation alone is to poorly consider the discipline. But this is exactly the case when an impoverished psychology is fervently separated from the humanities and then taken as a STEM (science, technology, engineering, mathematics) discipline—there is a movement to do so currently afoot in the American Psychological Association (Sipiora 2012a). Such a psychology, one in which the psyche is replaced by a computer model, is ugly. Hillman directs us to the greatest of Neoplatonist, Plotinus' definition of ugliness as "going over to another order" (1992, 59). When psychology is defined only as a natural science, conceived solely through calculation, and exclusively in terms of the computer model, it has gone over to another order—the causal order of the machine. It has left the order of the human by excluding the qualitative dimensions of human being and repressing the psyche.

Psychology is unthinkable without the humanities. A thoughtful psychology does not find it necessary to eschew causal explanation while it affirms interpretative understandings. Instead, a human science psychology, informed by the humanities, promotes dialogue with the natural sciences. A well-conceived psychology needs both calculation and imagination, both the natural sciences and the humanities.

CONCLUSION

The biographical-based personal reasons related in my professional narrative and the critically-generated, philosophical reasons articulated in my narrative of the profession, all argue that psychology is indeed unthinkable without the humanities. The humanities and the imagination of humanity—that is both its product and the source of that production—offer essential elements for a human science psychology that seeks to understand the meaningful experience of those who act and suffer. Without these elements, it would make no sense for me to be a psychologist.

As I noted in the preface to this essay, not only psychology is unthinkable without the humanities. So too are all the human sciences. Without the humanities, the human sciences are reduced to causal explanations that do cannot take into account the irreducible and integral nature of the qualitative dimensions of human experience and thus cannot account for meaning. When informed by the humanities, the human sciences bear witness to the power of imagination to disclose the human context and illuminate the realities that transcend explanation and call for another kind of understanding.

REFERENCES

Boss, Medard. 1988. "Recent Considerations in Daseinsanalysis." *Psychotherapy for Freedom: The Daseinsanalytical Way in Psychology and Psychoanalysis.* Ed. E. Craig. Spec. iss. of *The Humanistic Psychologist* 16.1: 58-74.

Brown, Norman O. 1959. *Life against Death: The Psychoanalytical Meaning of History.* New York: Random House.

———. 1966. *Love's Body.* New York: Random House.

Cushman, Peter. 1990. "Why the Self Is Empty: Toward a Historically Situated Social Psychology." *American Psychologist* 45.5: 599-611.

Giorgi, Amedeo. 1970. *Psychology as a Human Science: A Phenomenologically Based Approach.* New York: Harper and Row Publishers.

Heidegger, Martin. 1966. "Memorial Address." *Discourse on Thinking.* Trans. J. M. Anderson and E. H. Freund. New York: Harper and Row. 43-57.

———. 1968. *What Is Called Thinking?* Trans. J. Glenn Gray. New York: Harper and Row.

Hillman, James. 1975. *Re-Visioning Psychology.* New York: Harper and Row.

———. 1992. "The Thought of the Heart." *The Thought of the Heart and the Soul of the World.* Dallas: Spring Publications. 2-88.

May, Rollo. 1958. "The Origins and Significance of the Existential Movement in Psychology." *Existence: A New Dimension in Psychiatry and Psychology.* Ed. Ernest Angel, Henri F. Ellenberger, and Rollo May. New York: Basic Books. 3-36.

Ricoeur, Paul. 1991. "Life in Quest of Narrative." *On Paul Ricoeur: Narrative and interpretation.* Ed. David Wood. New York: Routledge. 22-33

Romanyshyn, Robert. 1989. *Technology as Symptom and Dream.* New York: Routledge, 1989.

Sipiora, Michael P. 1991. "Heidegger and Epideictic Discourse: The Rhetorical Performance of Meditative Thinking." *Philosophy Today* 4: 239-53.

———. 2000. "Psychology in the Neighborhood of Thought and Poetry: The Uncanny Logos of the Psyche." *Janus Head* 3.1: 40-61.

———. 2008. "Myth and Plot: Hillman and Ricoeur on Narrative." *Archetypal Psychologies.* Ed. Stanton Marlan. New Orleans: Spring Journal Books. 132-51.

———. 2012a. "Introduction: Psychology as a S.T.E.M. Discipline and As Logos of the Soul—The Critical Necessity of the Humanities for Psychological Science." *The Humanistic Psychologist* 40.4.

———. 2012b. "Sorrow, Existence, and the Humanities." *The Humanistic Psychologist* 40.4.

NO BROTHER LEFT BEHIND, NO SISTER LEFT BELOW: WINNING THE FUTURE BY TWINNING EDUCATION

Jennifer Leigh Selig

The first time President Barack Obama used the phrase, I had a visceral reaction, feeling literally pressed back into the couch as if the words had blown out of the television, a sudden and strange blast of hot air.

"Blah blah blah blah, **win the future.**"
Huh?
He did it again.
"Blah blah blah blah. **The future is ours to win.**"

On January 25th, 2011, during his State of the Union address, Obama encouraged and exhorted America, like an earnest basketball coach giving a locker room pep talk, to *win the future*, even laid out his game plan to *win the future*. He spoke this strange rhetorical phraseology five times in his speech, and each of those times, I had no idea what he meant. *How can the future be won?* The future is time, and time cannot be won (though if there was a lottery with time as the prize, I'd certainly purchase a ticket or two). And if we win the future, doesn't that mean others will lose the future? Is this the new American dream, to win the future at the expense of all other nations? Couldn't we share the future rather than compete for it? An image arose of a carnival worker plucking the largest stuffed whale off the wall and handing it to America, while other countries clutch their tiny goldfish and look at us with envy. *Step right up, and win the future.*

In poring over the text of the speech later in an attempt to penetrate this mysterious elocution, though I never came to understand *what* we would win or *why* we should win the future, it became clear to me *how* we would win it: by keeping our eyes on the prize of technology.

Obama's speech was laden with references to technology. He said, In a single generation, revolutions in technology have transformed the way we live, work and do business. Steel mills that once needed 1,000 workers can now do the same work with 100. Today, just about any company can set up shop, hire workers, and sell their products wherever there's an Internet connection.

Meanwhile, nations like China and India realized that with some changes of their own, they could compete in this new world. And so they started educating their children earlier and longer, with greater emphasis on math and science. They're investing in research and new technologies. Just recently, China became the home to the world's largest private solar research facility, and the world's fastest computer. (Obama 2011)

With a silicon chip on his shoulder, determined to defend against the competition from teams China and India, Obama laid out our offensive strategy.

The first step in winning the future is encouraging American innovation. None of us can predict with certainty what the next big industry will be or where the new jobs will come from. Thirty years ago, we couldn't know that something called the Internet would lead to an economic revolution. What we can do—what America does better than anyone else—is spark the creativity and imagination of our people. We're the nation that put cars in driveways and computers in offices; the nation of Edison and the Wright brothers; of Google and Facebook. In America, innovation doesn't just change our lives. It is how we make our living. (Obama 2011)

He continued, "Maintaining our leadership in research and technology is crucial to America's success. But if we want to win the future—if we want innovation to produce jobs in America and not overseas—then we also have to win the race to educate our kids." And that education, he told us, would heavily favor science and math, the twin legs upon which technology runs.

"Race to the Top" is the name of the Obama administration's educational agenda, replacing Bush's "No Child Left Behind." Bush's double negative horizontal metaphor was replaced with Obama's positive vertical metaphor. Where we once had a Texas rancher for a president who would herd up all the sheep, making sure none were left behind in the field, we now had a basketball coach for a president who would race us down the court to win the big game by slam dunking the ball over the top of the rim. The names on the backs of the shirts of the players: Google and Facebook.

Fifty years prior to this speech, America was poised to lose a race to the top known as "The Space Race." In the late 1950's and through the 1960's, America and Russia competed for the coveted prize of being the first country to launch a human into space. The Soviet Union won by orbiting Yuri Gagarin on April 12, 1961. It took America a full three weeks before it launched Alan Shepard. He missed the hoop; he failed to achieve orbit. It would be almost another year before astronaut John Glenn became the first American to orbit the Earth, on February 20, 1962 (NASA 2010).About a week after Gagarin's flight, President John F. Kennedy sent a memo to Vice President Lyndon B. Johnson, asking him to look into the state of America's space program, and into other programs that could offer the nation the opportunity to catch up, to even or better Russia's score. Yes, we had lost the space race, Johnson replied, but we could win the moon race (NASA n.d.). President Kennedy seized the challenge, and quite brilliantly, he redefined the game, resetting the score back to zero-zero. The real race, he told the world, would not be won by achieving space, but by landing a man on the moon. In what became known as his "We Choose to Go to the Moon" speech, he stated, "No nation which expects to be the leader of other nations can expect to stay behind in this race for space". The United States would *not be left behind* in this *race to the top*, and what's more, it would come, it *must* come, in first place. President Kennedy made the stakes of the game clear.

> Yet the vows of this Nation can only be fulfilled if we in this Nation are first, and, therefore, we intend to be first. We set sail on this new sea because there is new knowledge to be gained, and new rights to be won, and they must be won and used for the progress of all people. For space science, like nuclear science and all technology, has no conscience of its own. Whether it will become a force for good or ill depends on man, and only if the United States occupies a position of pre-eminence can we help decide whether this new ocean will be a sea of peace or a new terrifying theater of war. (Kennedy 1962)

The stakes of the game were nothing less than War and Peace; the names on the backs of the shirts of the players were Communism and Capitalism, and each team was terrified the other would toss the bomb down the court and slam dunk their respective countries into oblivion. In the Cold War, technology was both offense and defense; the twin bombs, Atom and Hydrogen, were mean players.

In the country's vapid pursuit of the first moon landing, in January of 1962 the United States introduced Project Gemini, a two-crew-member spacecraft that would eventually support Apollo by developing the key technologies of space rendezvous and docking of two craft with flight durations that would simulate going to the Moon and back. Project Gemini launched ten missions between 1965 and 1966 (NASA 2000).

Between the time of Project Gemini's conception and birth, I was conceived and born, a double Gemini, sun and moon in the sign. My life is marked by the mythological twins, Castor and Pollux. Born of the same mother, they had two different fathers, one mortal, one immortal, making Pollux the immortal twin, and Castor the mortal one. When Castor died, Pollux asked Zeus to let him share his own immortality with his beloved twin to keep them together, and they were transformed into the Gemini constellation.

Pollux didn't want to leave Castor behind. Pollux didn't want to race to the top of the world while Castor was relegated to the underworld. This is a story of brotherly love, two twins living side by side in the cosmos, cooperative, not competitive.

There was no brotherly love in the 50's and 60's between America and Russia, and there was no cooperation, only competition. In a sign of national humility that is hard to imagine today, President Kennedy admitted that his was the country left behind in the space race. In his "We Choose to Go to the Moon" speech, he stated, "To be sure, we are behind, and will be behind for some time in manned flight. But we do not intend to stay behind, and in this decade, we shall make up and move ahead" (Kennedy 1962).

The location where Kennedy gave his speech was important. It was at Rice University, a technical institution in Houston, Texas, which had just crowned Kennedy as an honorary visiting professor. On that blazingly hot day in late summer of 1962, Professor Kennedy declared that we would win the Cold War not by being left behind (we would not "flounder in the backwash") but by racing to the top ("space is there, and we're going to climb it") (Kennedy 1962). The game plan to win the Cold War was to come in first in the space race, thus winning the right to lead the future. Our educational system, already the whipping boy back then for everything wrong with our country, was blamed for our loss thus far, but on its back was also placed the power to win back the future. Plans were already underway to bolster our national technological prowess through strengthening those twin legs upon which technology runs: math and science. The United States' National Defense Education Act of 1958 increased funding for these goals from childhood education through the post-graduate level (U.S. Department of Education 2011).

Education was twinned with Defense in that act of 1958 and in President/Professor Kennedy's subsequent speech in 1962 on defense at an educational institution. Kennedy linked "our leadership in science and industry" and "our hopes for peace and security" with "the growth of our science and education" (Kennedy). Education was framed and understood as critical to national security. The nation was at risk; education was the difference between life and death, between mortality and immortality. If a humanities education must be left behind in favor of a technological education, surely the stakes warranted the one-legged approach.

What was at stake nearly 50 years later, when President Obama gave his "We Will Win the Future" speech? Why did he call this "our Sputnik moment," and promise to fund "the Apollo projects of our time"? Why did he tell the country that we need "to reach a level of research and development we haven't seen since the height of the Space Race" (Obama 2011)?. Why was this mortal brother, Obama, echoing the language of his immortal brother, Kennedy, in calling for a focus on technology, on science and math, as a means of winning this race to the top?

The answer no longer lied in national security. It lied in something else entirely.

After we won the race to put a man on the moon in 1969 through the educational push for more math and science, there was a backlash of progressive education in the late 1960's and into the 1970's. The Open Education Movement or Open Classroom Movement focused on student-centered rather than curriculum-centered education, and much of the education featured the humanities (Cuban 2011). I entered school during those years. My school did not emphasize rote learning; I remember a little math and very little science but lots of reading, lots of literature, lots of history. We sat on rugs; there was art everywhere; we performed plays; we made a lot of dioramas and gave reports on history's heroes; we wrote on the walls; we moved through learning centers and when we finished our work, we could reward ourselves by returning to the center of our choosing; we were encouraged to find and follow our own bliss in the classroom. I was neither pushed to the top nor left behind; I was taught to cooperate with my classmates, not to compete. And while some parents complained that the school was far too lax, I remember feeling encouraged to challenge myself.

The sense of laxity led to the back-to-the-basics movement, where reading, writing, and arithmetic were stressed. There was too much freedom and indiscretion in our schools, so we got off the rugs and into our desks, got straightened up and serious again about education. In 1983, the National Commission on Excellence in Education published the report *A Nation at Risk* with its message that America was again in peril (U.S. National Commission on Excellence in Education 1983). It was no longer our national security but our economic security at stake, as the United States was falling behind such superpowers as Japan, Germany, and Korea, unable to compete with them economically. Education was once again the whipping boy, technology was once again extolled, and math and science were once again exalted as the keys to victory. We were falling behind in test scores, so test scores would be emphasized. The movement away from open education and toward standardization began, and reforms through the 1980's and 1990's led directly to the "No Child Left Behind" policy where The Test was the uber-measure of all things excellent (Education Week 2004). Once again the humanities were swept ignominiously out the back doors of our schools; if not part of the problem, they were definitely not part of the solution.

Out the back door the humanities are still huddled, the mortal twin who dies a little death or is at least left gasping for breath each time technology is resurrected as the winning strategy. In a repeat of the pattern of the 1980's, in 2011 when Obama raised technology to god-like status, it was not in the name of national security, but rather, national prosperity. The competition, as Kennedy framed it in the 1960's, was for knowledge that would lead to a peaceful future. The completion, as Obama framed it, was for jobs that would lead to a prosperous future. He told the nation, "The competition for jobs is real. But this shouldn't discourage us. It should challenge us. Remember—for all the hits we've taken these last few years, for all the naysayers predicting our decline, America still has the largest, most prosperous economy in the world" (Obama 2011). And to keep it that way, to ensure we would win the future, Technology would be the captain of our team, with Math and Science the point-guards. Humanities was benched for the game.

Perhaps as a double Gemini, it is my lot to root for the underdog. When the sun shines, I root for the moon. When the moon rises, I root for the sun. With Obama a cheerleader on the television for Team Technology, I became a cheerleader on the couch for Team Humanities. When Obama called, "We need to teach our kids that it's not just the winner of the Super Bowl who deserves to be celebrated, but the winner of the science fair" (Obama 2011), this Gemini responded, "What about the winner of the poetry contest?" When Obama called, "And over the next 10 years, with so many baby boomers retiring from our classrooms, we want to prepare 100,000 new teachers in the fields of science and technology and engineering and math," this Gemini responded, "What about 100,000 new teachers in the fields of art and literature and history and culture?" When Obama called the American Dream a dream of prosperity, this Gemini recalled an earlier leader who called the American Dream a dream of equality.

In all likelihood, I was conceived right around the time when Martin Luther King, Jr. delivered his galvanizing "I Have a Dream" speech. I like to imagine that the hot August air in 1963 on my young parents' college campus was infused with the electricity from that King's speech, and they coupled under the constellations, letting their "freedom ring from the curvaceous slopes of California." In that speech, King borrowed from the Bible when he stated, "I have a dream that one day every valley shall be exalted, every hill and mountain shall be made low, the rough places will be made plain, and the crooked places will be made straight, and the glory of the Lord shall be revealed, and all flesh shall see it together" (King 1963). These natural images of equality remove the horizontal and vertical planes which privilege top over bottom, ahead over behind, us over them. There is no competition, only cooperation; *we all* shall see the glory of God. This was King's vision of how we would win the future—together. Both Castor and Pollux will make it to the Promised Land, no brother (or sister) left behind, no brother (or sister) left below.

King came of age during the Cold War; he spoke these words during the Space Race-turned-Moon Race. He knew the marvels of technology, and extolled them often in some of his most eloquent and poetic passages.

Modern man has brought this whole world to an awe-inspiring threshold of the future. He has reached new and astonishing peaks of scientific success. He has produced machines that think and instruments that peer into the unfathomable ranges of interstellar space. He has built gigantic bridges to span the seas and gargantuan

107

buildings to kiss the skies. His airplanes and spaceships have dwarfed distance, placed time in chains, and carved highways through the stratosphere. This is a dazzling picture of modern man's scientific and technological progress. (King 1964)

However, he noted,

In spite of these spectacular strides in science and technology, and still unlimited ones to come, something basic is missing. There is a sort of poverty of the spirit which stands in glaring contrast to our scientific and technological abundance. The richer we have become materially, the poorer we have become morally and spiritually. We have learned to fly the air like birds and swim the sea like fish, but we have not learned the simple art of living together as brothers. (ibid.)

He told America, "Through our scientific and technological genius we've made of this world a neighborhood. And now through our moral and ethical commitment we must make of it a brotherhood. We must all learn to live together as brothers—or we will all perish together as fools" (King 1965). Both Castor and Pollux would live together as immortals or they would both perish together as mortals. And how would they survive and thrive? Through the twinning of science and morality; through the twinning of technology and ethics. Yet, he noted, "Our scientific power has outrun our spiritual power. We have guided missiles and misguided men"(King 1963b, 76).

And what would guide men?

Each of us lives in two realms, the internal and the external. The internal is that realm of spiritual ends expressed in art, literature, morals, and religion. The external is that complex of devices, techniques, mechanisms, and instrumentalities by means of which we live. . . . There is always a danger that we will permit the means by which we live to replace the ends for which we live, the internal to become lost in the external. (King 1963b, 70)

Stated another way, we have allowed the external means of technology to overcome the internal ends expressed in the humanities, through art, literature, morals, religion, philosophy, history, and language. King admonished us not be misguided and believe "Technology shall overcome one day." Our humanity must run as fast as our technology, if not faster.

We have allowed the means by which we live to outdistance the ends for which we live. So much of modern life can be summarized in that arresting dictum of the poet Thoreau: "Improved means to an unimproved end." This is the serious predicament, the deep and haunting problem confronting modern man. . . When the "without" of man's nature subjugates the "within," dark storm clouds begin to form in the world. (King 1964)

King had lived through dark storm clouds, the mushroom clouds of Hiroshima and Nagasaki that forever stain America's soul. With its insatiable need to be first, America dropped the twin bombs, slam-dunks from the sky, and the innocuously-named teammates Fat Man and Little Boy changed the game forever, causing us to question what is offense, and what is defense?

Though Fat Man and Little Boy had many sperm donors, they were the main prodigy of scientist Robert Oppenheimer. Oppenheimer, Algis Valiunas argued in his essay "The Agony of an Atomic Genius," was caught in a strange time period where the definition of a scientist was changing.

Under Vannevar Bush [the M.I.T. engineer who sold the Manhattan Project to President Roosevelt], the scientist as the enlightened keeper of cultural ideals and an equal partner with military and political leaders was replaced by a new conception of the scientist as a mere technician of physical processes, an employee working under orders at the bottom of a bureaucratic hierarchy. (Valiunas 2006)

"The enlightened keeper of cultural ideas"—in other words, the humanitarian—was replaced by "the scientist as a mere technician . . . an employee" doing work for hire. Whereas scientists were once "revered as white knights consecrated to the cosmopolitan ideals of perpetual peace, [and] rapturous discovery in the name of humankind," increasingly their discoveries were commissioned by the nation-state, in the name of the nation-state, which was synonymous with the military. At first, Valiunas reported, Oppenheimer was not eager to give his intelligence over to the war effort, but for various "tangled and complex" reasons of his own, including a partly egoic, partly humanitarian desire to win honor and renown to his name for having made the weapon that would save civilization, Oppenheimer turned over his knowledge to his nation. His twin sons Fat Man and Little Boy live in infinity, while they rendered one hundred thousand times as many of God's children instantly finite (Valiunas 2006).

Before his sons were unleashed, Oppenheimer wrote in a letter to a friend, "I have a lot more misgivings even than you ever had about what will come of all this; but even so I think surely if I were asked to do a job I could do really well and that needed doing I'd not refuse. I'd worry a lot, perhaps even more than you. But we worry anyway" (quoted in Valiunas 2006). In his inner struggle between the scientist as humanitarian and technician, Oppenheimer as the dutiful and proficient employee won out.

Oppenheimer was by all accounts a conflicted man, both proud of what his intellectual power produced, yet horrified by the ends it had been put to, even as he must have known the probability that his means would be put to that end. After the bombs were dropped, he kept repeating of the Japanese victims, "Those poor little people, those poor little people". His pride gave way to terrible guilt and despair, and when he later met President Truman, he said, "Mr. President, I feel I have blood on my hands." According to legend, Truman handed him a handkerchief and asked him if he would like to wipe his hands. After Oppenheimer left, Truman called him a "cry-baby scientist" and "insisted that nuclear war be conducted without tears" (Valiunus 2006).

Oppenheimer spoke out during his life about the bomb. In an address to the American Philosophical Society, he stated, "We have made a thing, a most terrible weapon, that has altered abruptly and profoundly the nature of the world . . . a thing that by all the standards of the world we grew up in is an evil thing. And by so doing . . . we have raised again the question of whether science is good for man" (quoted in Valiunus 2006).

We can argue about whether the atom bomb saved more lives than it cost; we can argue about whether the threat of nuclear annihilation has ultimately been good for the world, making all wars since World War II relatively tame by comparison in terms of loss of life. What we can't argue, however, is that science is always good for man, that technological advances are always good for humanity. Horrible experiments have been done in the name of science; horrible results have been wrought in the name of technology. C. G. Jung, in his essay "The Effect of Technology on the Human Psyche" wrote, "Considered on its own merits, as a legitimate human activity, technology is neither good nor bad, neither harmful nor harmless. Whether it be used for good or ill depends entirely on man's own attitude" (Jung 1949, 615). This calls to mind Kennedy's statement that "technology has no conscience of its own. Whether it will become a force for good or ill depends on man" (Kennedy) and Albert Einstein's acknowledgement that "technological progress is like an axe in the hands of a pathological criminal" (Einstein 1946).

Inside of the conscience of its creator, the atom bomb had become a force for ill (Oppenheimer came to believe that Japan was ultimately already a defeated enemy), and he was wracked with guilt and despair that grew deeper over time. Valiunas writes,

> Years later he would remember thinking to himself as he saw the towering cloud of the blast, "Now I am become death, the destroyer of worlds"—a quotation from his beloved *Bhagavad Gita*, in which the god Vishnu exhorts Prince Arjuna to do his duty and pursue martial greatness. This quotation would be enshrined as Oppenheimer's signature line, and as the expression of inconsolable regret. (Valiunus 2006)

The fact that Oppenheimer was able to feel regret came in part from his studies of the humanities, which he combined with his study of science. He learned Sanskrit so he could read the classic Indian religious literature, searching for wisdom that values-neutral science couldn't provide him (Valiunas 2006). He was critiqued for this by some in the scientific community, as if it were a weakness. American physicist and Nobel laureate Isidor Isaac Rabi stated, "In some respects Oppenheimer was overeducated in those fields that lie outside the scientific tradition, such as his interest in religion, in the Hindu religion in particular, which resulted in a feeling for the mystery of the universe that surrounded him almost like a fog" (quoted in ibid).

This statement is both fascinating and frightening, suggesting that any education in the humanities is "overeducation" to the scientist, likely to cause a foggy mind. Einstein disagreed. He wrote,

> It is not enough to teach a man a specialty. Through it he may become a kind of useful machine, but not a harmoniously developed personality. It is essential that the student acquire an understanding of and a lively feeling for values. He must acquire a vivid sense of the beautiful and of the morally good. . . . He must learn to understand the motives of human beings, their illusions and their sufferings, in order to acquire a proper relationship to individual fellow men and to the community. (Einstein 1954)

And where are these qualities developed, acquired, learned? Through an education in the humanities. Depth psychologist C. G. Jung noted the importance of a balanced education as well. He wrote, "The technologist has something of the same problem as the faculty worker. Since he has to do mainly with mechanical factors, there is a danger of his other mental capacities atrophying." His recommendation was to create "Humanistic Faculties" in the polytechnic institutions (Jung 1949, 615). Twin a technological education with one in the humanities.

I hear Einstein's call for us to acquire a proper relationship to others in the community when I hear Obama's speech, and I can't believe that snatching the future out of everyone else's hands is a proper relationship. Nor will teaching everyone to be math and science specialists make us into Einstein's harmoniously developed personalities. I can't accept that the goal of our education should be to win the future, to "out-innovate, out-educate, and out-build the rest of the world," in Obama's words (Obama 2011). Instead, I adhere to Martin Luther King, Jr.'s definition of the goal of education.

> We must remember that intelligence is not enough. Intelligence plus character—that is the goal of true education. The complete education gives one not only power of concentration, but worthy objectives upon which to concentrate. The broad education will, therefore, transmit to one not only the accumulated knowledge of the race but also the accumulated experience of social living. (King 1963b)

The humanities hold "the accumulated experience of social living," while technology, standing on the twin legs of math and science, holds" the accumulated knowledge of the race." America does not need to be the master race, nor does it need to win the race; I would prefer it to hold court as a team player. On the backs of the shirts of the players on King's team are Intelligence and Character. Technology in brotherhood with the humanities can increase both our national intelligence and our national character, and in turn make the international community a much nicer neighborhood in which to live. The humanities are the limbs of education that grow the soul, express the spirit, and contain the repository of human wisdom, the storehouse of our grand experiment in social living, offering a place to discuss the ends for which we live. In the humanities reside the big questions—what makes life worth living? What values should shape the life of the individual and the life of the nation?—and in the humanities we learn the critical thinking tools we need to engage the questions and begin to discern, articulate, and apply our answers. Technology may be the two legs we stand upon, but the humanities are our two arms, able to reach out and transform a neighborhood into a brotherhood. We will all win the future if we let both have their place in the stars.

No brother left behind, no sister left below.

REFERENCES

Cuban, Larry. 2001. "The Open Classroom." *Education Next* 23 (Oct.). http//educationnext.org/theopenclassroom, accessed 20 September 2011.

Education Week. 2004. "No Child Left Behind." *Education Week,* 4 August. <http://www.edweek.org/ew/issues/no-child-left-behind/>. Accessed 17 August 2011.

Einstein, Albert. 1946. Albert Einstein to Raymond Benenson, 31 January 1946. Reprinted in *The Ultimate Quotable Einstein.* Ed. Alice Calaprice. Princeton: Princeton U Press, 2011. 397.

———. 1952. "Education for Independent Thought." *New York Times,* 5 Oct. 1952. Republished in Einstein, *Ideas and Opinions: Based on Mein Weltbild.* New York: Crown Publishers, 1954.

Jung, C. G. 1949. "The Effect of Technology on the Human Psyche." *The Symbolic Life: Miscellaneous Writings.* Princeton: Princeton U Press, 1949. 614-615.

Kennedy, John F. 1962. "John F. Kennedy Moon Speech—Rice Stadium." 12 Sept. 1962. <http://er.jsc.nasa.gov/seh/ricetalk.htm>. Accessed 4 June 2011.

King, Martin Luther, Jr. 1963a. "I Have a Dream." 28 August 1963. The Avalon Project: Documents in Law, History, and Diplomacy. <http://avalon.law.yale.edu/20th_century/mlk01.asp>. Accessed 7 January 2012.

———. 1963b. "The Man Who Was a Fool." *Strength to Love.* Philadelphia: Fortress Press, 1963. 69-76.

———. 1964. "Nobel Lecture." 11 December 1964. Nobelprize.org. <http://www.nobelprize.org/nobel_prizes/peace/laureates/1964/king-lecture.html>. Accessed 15 November 2011.

———. 1965. "Remaining Awake Through a Great Revolution." June 1965. Oberlin College Archives. <http://www.oberlin.edu/external/EOG/BlackHistoryMonth/MLK/CommAddress.html>. Accessed 15 November 2011.

NASA. 2000. "Project Gemini." 25 August. <http://science.ksc.nasa.gov/history/gemini/gemini.html>. Accessed 9 June 2011.

———. 2010. "Sputnik and the Dawn of the Space Age."10 October. <http://history.nasa.gov/sputnik/>. Accessed 4 June 2011.

———. N.d. "Project Apollo: A Retrospective Analysis." <http://history.nasa.gov/Apollomon/Apollo.html>. Accessed 5 June 2011.

Obama, Barack. 2011. "Remarks by the President in State of the Union Address." 12 June 2011. The White House: President Barack Obama.

<http://www.whitehouse.gov/the-press-office/2011/01/25/remarks-president-state-union-address>. Accessed 7 January 2012.

U.S. Department of Education. 2011. "The Federal Role in Education." 30 March. <http://www2.ed.gov/about/overview/fed/role.html>. Accessed 3 July 2011.

U.S. National Commission on Excellence in Education. 1983. *A Nation at Risk: The Imperative for Educational Reform: A Report to the Nation and the Secretary of Education.* Washington, DC: National Commission on Excellence in Education.

Valiunas, Algis. 2006. "The Agony of an Atomic Genius." *The New Atlantis* (Fall). <http://www.thenewatlantis.com/publications/the-agony-of-atomic-genius>. Accessed 24 June 2011

AN EXPANDED DEFINITION OF A HUMANITIES EDUCATION

Gwyn Wood

I believed, after my first semester in college, that I had been tricked. I had chosen to major in Chemistry at a Bay Area university well known for student activism during the 60's, a naked man who roamed campus and scientists who rigged their fire alarms to lab equipment to notify the whole campus, and the fire department, when they created a new element for the periodic table.

This choice flew in the face of my upbringing; I left behind a childhood home stacked to the rafters with novels, art projects, dog-eared copies of journal articles, canisters of film, and a vinyl music collection which had my hipster friends whistling and reappraising the coolness factor of parents. I spent my formative years reading, viewing, and listening to everything in that house. I was raised by an English teacher and Librarian; the art and language of human creation were a part of our everyday lives. We projected silent films onto the dining room wall, watching Charlie Chaplin pushed through the cogs of a machine in *Modern Times* during winter dinners. Every summer my father would throw two pairs of Osh-Kosh overalls and a toothbrush into a suitcase for me and head for the airport. We travelled all over the world: one July would be South Africa, the next Peru—as he worked on his oral history projects. I read Hemingway, Hawthorne and the love letters of Napoleon and Josephine in the dusky autumn afternoons in my tree house, supplied with helpful notes—"ask yourself why Hester Prynne agreed to wear the scarlet A"—my mother left on the fridge in the morning. We painted a timeline of major events in western history on the outside of my father's crumbling Victorian for Halloween one year after the neighborhood association begged him to spruce up the house. I was allowed to paint a large hammer and sickle in red to commemorate the Russian Revolution of 1917 in a spot which corresponded with the beginning of the porch and a large rocket ship on our front door for the Apollo moon landing. Things became a bit cloudy for my understanding, and our timeline, when we began to add arrows theorizing causality between major events—did the kitchen window's ode to the end of the British slave trade really need a 9 foot pink arrow to the garage's American Civil War years?—but it was a grand introduction to history. I headed off to college convinced I had learned everything I could from the humanities, certain science was the next step to understanding the world.

My short-lived career in science, and eventual degrees in Film and History, taught me that I already held the keys to the kingdom. I learned three things which gave me perspective into the traditional dividing lines we are taught to expect between an education in the humanities and one in the sciences. First and foremost, education addresses the big questions of human existence; the paths used to pursue this knowledge may vary by major but the quest is the same. Second, the content and methodologies considered sacred to the humanities the study of language, story, culture and art are alive and well in a wide variety of disciplines. Last, an education within the humanities leads one to a unique position to delve deeper into the "big questions" of life as students study the mediums through which we address these questions. I managed to trick myself by believing there was a fundamental difference in the humanities-based knowledge I had acquired through my childhood and what I would learn in a university chemistry program.

THE BIG QUESTIONS

Throughout my first term of college I realized the lessons I had learned from novels, from history, and from art were all present in the chemistry lectures I attended and the physics labs I slaved over. As teaching assistants guided us through the basics of balancing equations, I wondered how this was different from a Religious Studies course. While balancing the equation for photosynthesis I could take three oxygen atoms from one side of the chemical reaction, redistribute them to account for transformation and then find balance on the other side of the arrow. The professors told me matter was finite, change occurred and the universe demanded balance. This was the same lecture I had heard when studying Hinduism although some of the vocabulary just happened to be different. Exchange the term *reactant* for that of *prakiti* (matter, creative energy) and the idea was the same. The larger "truth" that lay beneath an exquisitely balanced chemical equation was analogous to the knowledge that a careful reading of the *Mahabharata* could yield.

Students end up in a department studying, learning, and living with a type of knowledge for four or more years. Whether students tackle coursework in biology, business, or literature the driving questions underneath the discipline's specific goals ask eternal questions that relate to our understanding of ourselves as a species, our purpose in life and our relationship with the world we live in. I believed an education in the sciences would definitively answer the big questions: "Who are we?" "What is the meaning of life?" "What is the world we live in?" that I had encountered in countless novels, philosophies and films during my childhood, and provide a new series of questions to ponder. I thought the humanities asked the questions while science could answer them. I soon learned the same questions and truths could be found in the study of matter as well as glimpsed within the harvest of words and images that constitute the arts.

As my first semester continued, the lessons of biology were eerily familiar as well. As I studied at coffee shops I would chant the names of bones, organs and ligaments while flipping through note cards in the manner of a meditative Catholic with her rosary. The lessons beneath the surface of this science resonated with me: structures connect every living being, whether on the singular level: the musculature of a mammalian foot that made movement possible, or the macro: the complex social web of a 19th century village in George Eliot's *Middlemarch*. The Achilles tendon joining the plantaris muscle to the calcaneus heel bone was just as elegant and balanced an arrangement to support life as the social responsibilities and power structures which joined the landed gentry, emerging middle class and working poor within Eliot's imagined world.

In anatomy class we dissected a fetal pig. As my scalpel sliced through layers of intestine and I held the piglet's innards within my gloved hand, I reencountered the same lesson I learned from Joseph Heller's satirical novel, *Catch-22*, all those years ago in my tree house. Heller's anti-hero protagonist, Yossarian, an American bomber in the WWII Air Force, encounters a fatality early in his tour of duty and spends the rest of the novel desperately trying to avoid active service and the inherent risk of being shot out of the sky. In the passage below Snowden, a young gunner wounded during an aerial attack, bleeds out in Yossarian's lap as the pilot desperately tries to get them all back to base and medical help.

He [Yossarian] felt goose pimples clacking all over him as he gazed down despondently at the grim secret Snowden had spilled all over the messy floor. It was easy to read the message in his entrails. Man was matter, that was Snowden's secret. Drop him out a window and he'll fall. Set fire to him and he'll burn. Bury him and he'll rot, like other kinds of garbage. The spirit gone, man is garbage. That was Snowden's secret. Ripeness was all. (Heller 1955, 440)

Heller's words, and the fetal pig's guts, presented a striking materialist argument for understanding mortality. Both experiences provided a possible answer for that tricky "meaning of life" question we all ponder. Snowden's fictional death and the pig's actual passing contained the same essential lessons. Yes, we all die. Yes, we are biological beings, and ripeness is all. There might not be more than our guts once the spirit is gone, and this might be the epiphany Snowden and the pig reveal. Just as ancient Greeks and Romans would try to read the future within the entrails of animals on the sacrificial altar, we too can examine Snowden's guts for clues to our own mortality, our own world and our own fear. A biology lab and a novel can reveal the same lesson.

I do not deny that a dissection laboratory will impart different information than a novel can supply. Future doctors and researchers should study the anatomy of animals so that they may stitch us all back together when we are ill and explore the boundaries of biology. This detailed knowledge will not be something a medical student encounters in a literature class. Conversely, a writer must achieve mastery of character, pace, and syntax in order to weave together story. These are not lessons to be found with a scalpel. However, the deeper questions which drive medicine and art—the eternal "whys" and "hows" of life—inform both disciplines and can be glimpsed in the pursuit of any type of knowledge.

In my science courses the professors would speak in the language of story and metaphor when presenting a new theory. Einstein's theory of relativity might be encapsulated in an elegant few letters, $E=mc^2$, but no one understood what this meant until we heard the story of Einstein's revelation and identified the concepts or ideas which each letter and number stood for. Time and space were not discrete entities within the physical world; they interacted with one another, creating tension and constriction in the universe. The class blinked at this, but comprehension began when the professor moved into metaphor, explaining the "dance" time and space wove in and out of when they encountered matter and energy. Most of us had a solid grasp of the material once an elaborate deconstruction of the *Back to the Future* movies had eaten away two lectures. They spoke in the language of story in order to teach.

Later in my academic career I joined a Social Psychology research lab. Many experiments in this field rely on manufactured social encounters within the laboratory setting and careful observation of participants' reactions. Say a test subject agrees to participate in a cognitive reaction time study where they're asked to respond to words or colors on the screen. As this person walks down the hall to enter the computer lab where the "experiment" will occur, someone pops out of a door and drops a handful of pencils (Latané and Dabbs 1975). The real experiment occurs in this twenty or so seconds, even though the participant will spend half an hour looking at a screen and giving feedback after the encounter with the pencil dropper. The study, in this case, is about generosity and helpfulness—how many people will stop to help pick up the pencils? How many seconds does it take before they respond? Will more people help pick up the pencils if the pencil dropper is male, female, of the same ethnic group as the subject? These are all variables that the researchers would be interested in. Their "big question" delved into understanding why humans display selfless behavior when there might not be evolutionary benefit in doing so.

On my first day the professor who ran the lab gave me a handout which was a quick and dirty summary of the dramatic structure of plays. Gustav Freytag's (2011) 5 stages—exposition, rising action, climax, falling action and dénouement—were all present in the triangle diagram any literature student would instantly recognize. To this day I'm not sure if any of the research personnel in the lab had ever heard of Freytag or knew the background of his theories, firmly rooted within a critique of Aristotle's definition of drama and plot. The psychology cliff notes version of his work had a brief description of each stage with a handwritten aside after each, photocopied within an inch of legibility. The exposition, or explanation, stage was: "the advertisement for research subjects," while the rising action corresponded to the set-up within the lab, the climax was the "response to stimuli" while the dénouement extended into the debriefing session all research subjects went through after their part in the experiment was over. There was a question mark and a hastily scribbled remark next to "dénouement" that appeared to question the sanity of using a funny French word for what can also be called the resolution stage. The Psychology professor told me most good research scenarios followed this dramatic structure and that I learn them in order to have an understanding of how social science research functioned. His graduate students through the years have gone on to run their own labs, each venturing into the world with their photocopy of a German author's 19th century analysis of Shakespearean and classic Greek drama. I would argue all of these social scientists received a thorough grounding in the Humanities, whether they were aware of it or not.

SEARCHING UNDERNEATH

Within traditional Humanities disciplines there might lie a layer of analysis in our quest for answers not immediately available to those in the sciences. To study literature, film, art, philosophy or culture is to pursue the "who are we?" "why are we here" questions while taking the quest one step further. To create or critique a cultural text, a student must understand the medium itself and ponder why the questions are asked. The research questions reach beyond "why are we here?" to ponder: "how is it that we ask and partially answer that question for generations of humans with a story they relate to?" and "why do we, as a species, need to ask why we are here?" Biology, physics, chemistry—they teach their students to examine the first question and supply marvelous answers that are vital to our understanding of the world. Students in the Humanities delve several levels deeper as they examine the mediums through which possible answers are delivered and the motivation for asking those questions in the first place.

A modern understanding of this phenomenon can be found in the work of the German filmmaker Werner Herzog. In his Minnesota Declaration he writes, "… in the fine arts, in music, literature, and cinema, it is possible to reach a deeper stratum of truth—a poetic, ecstatic truth, which is mysterious and can only be grasped with effort; one attains it through vision, style, and craft" (Herzog 1999). Plato touched upon this in his dialogues (Plato 360 B.C.), arguing the theory of "Forms" or ideas as the highest and most fundamental conveyers of reality. In his estimation, true knowledge can only emerge from a study of the Forms, rather than through sensations and data from the physical world. While also expressing mistrust for both shadow representations of reality and those who wielded that storytelling power in his "Allegory of the Cave", Plato clearly valued the philosophical over the material, just as Herzog believes deep truth comes from artifice (manipulation of the physical world).

Herzog often uses Michelangelo's Pietà as a prime example of this theory. The famous sculpture portrays Mary cradling the body of her dead son after the Crucifixion. The sculpture evokes an intense emotional response in spectators "making possible an ecstatic experience of inner, deeper truth" as Herzog describes it (Herzog 1999). Michelangelo's work is deceptive: the figure of Jesus is abnormally small in order to accommodate his placement in Mary's lap and the Virgin is depicted as a youthful adolescent, remarkably younger than her son.

I saw the sculpture for the first time when I was a teenager, being dragged by my father through every museum, cathedral and palace from Paris to Rome. I was fourteen years old and had looked at hundreds of paintings, walked through miles of abbeys, cathedrals and palaces and was not prepared to have the Pietà pierce my cloud of weariness and apathy. I stood in St. Peter's Basilica and had my own moment of sublime truth. Michelangelo's Mary cradles Jesus in her lap as though he were still an infant. The serene and loving gaze she rests upon her son's broken body is not a comment upon the prophet he will become or the terrible nature of his death. The body in her lap is that of the infant Jesus, for whom the Wise Men gathered, innocent and full of promise. Mary sees this version of her son, while the sculpture's audience takes in the nature of his death. Both of these stages; the infant messiah and the savior who greets death willingly, are key to an understanding of the Jesus figure. These elements suggest deeper truths surrounding this significant moment in the Judeo Christian tradition which eliminate the element of fakery when Michelangelo's Pietà portrays Jesus as a 33-year-old man, and his mother, the mother of God, as a 17-year-old. Michelangelo's manipulation of the marble, his figures, and his audience make this revelation possible. The artist's "deception" reveals a complex truth.

Consider then, an art student's study of Michelangelo's work. Students in the arts must consider the meaning of the sculpture, and the piece's ability to elicit a response within a viewer. This is one level of study. Those who study within the arts have the opportunity to experience these moments of ecstatic truth while also studying the mechanisms of the stories and images which, through their very artifice, are able to connect the audience with the sublime. The construction of stories, whether through words or image, rests primarily within the domain of the humanities. These mediums have mastered the presentation of ecstatic truths and act as unique containers in which to explore fictional worlds and, by extension, ourselves. The distance fictional perspectives can give us provide perspective to examine our own lives and worlds and enough freedom from consequence to ponder the uncomfortable questions of mortality.

RECONSIDERING A HUMANITIES EDUCATION

The debate over the value of a humanities education continues in our culture. These debates are held at the public level—a social conversation mediated by the media and policy makers such as the ongoing discussion over funding the Endowment for the Arts within the United States. The dialogue continues, and shapes much of the eventual public discourse, within the ivory tower of academia. The value of arts and humanities research is a hotly debated issue within universities. The valorization of academic research over the past fifty years has influenced the funding of different departments, and the perception of which disciplines offer a worthy education to undergraduates.

With the advent of the Cold War and the subsequent technology race in the west, university research became inexorably tied to government and private funding. National governments looked to universities to make their economies competitive through the development of new pharmaceutical drugs, bio-technology patents, defense research and other technological innovations. This was especially true from the 1980's forward after the implementation of the Bayh-Dole Act, a patent law which linked the technology transfer between universities and the private sector while allowing educational institutions to hold the patents and seed the profit from these innovations into the university systems' long term budgets. Thus, the perception of "value" in intellectual research moved away from broad perceptions of societal value to be understood as primarily economic. This valorization model favors the hard sciences over the arts; the development of Nano processers over the advancement of the arts; the classroom dissection of a fetal pig over teaching Joseph Heller's work. As departmental funding shifted to favor the sciences in western universities, cultural perceptions about how to assess the value of education also shifted.

Many students choose their college majors today with future possible earnings in mind. The "value" of an education is now calculated in dollars, rather than knowledge and skills amassed. While an undergraduate, my academic advisor retold the threadbare joke that a degree in film theory would qualify me to ask "Would you like fries with that?" when I graduated. While economic and professional concerns are certainly valid criteria to consider when choosing a discipline to study, these are not the only standards. One way to reframe this debate is to reassess the value of research in the arts and humanities. Dr. Paul Benneworth, a researcher at the University of Twente, notes "The measures that we have fail to capture what really matters about arts and humanities research." This framing of value is a disservice to all areas of study—the "truths" glimpsed within each discipline and the ability for original thought and development cannot be captured by a dollar sign. The economic definition of value within academic research has come to define the undergraduate experience as well. It is time to reframe the question of value in education to include the interpretive as well as the economic.

The eternal big questions are present in all disciplines; the quest for "truth" within all academic programs of study is the same across departments. A science major asks the same questions a literature student might, and will often use the tools of story, metaphor and symbols to answer those questions. The methodologies and content of the humanities—art, literature, critical study of culture and language, are present, if often unacknowledged, in all the sciences, be they social or physical. My eventual educational path led through the Humanities, with stops in Film and History, but I have assimilated the lessons I learned in the sciences along the way. I can appreciate the beauty and meaning present in a well-crafted story and a well-reasoned theorem. Both hold an understanding of our lives and our world, and both hold value.

REFERENCES

Benner, Paul. 2011. "HERAVALUE Roundtable Discussion: The Value of Arts and Humanities Research in Society." Ashe Conference, Dublin Technology Institute, Dublin, Ireland, November 22.

Freytag, Gustav. 2010. *Freytag's Technique of the Drama; An Exposition of Dramatic Composition and Art*. New York: General Books.

Heller, Joseph. 1955. *Catch-22*. New York: Simon and Schuster.

Herzog, Werner. 1999. "Minnesota Declaration: Truth and Fact in Documentary Cinema." Lecture/presentation after a screening, Milan, Italy. April 30. <http://www.walkerart.org/magazine/1999/minnesota-declaration-truth-and-fact-in-docum>. Accessed 7 January 2012.

Latané, Bibb, and James M. Dabbs. 1975. "Sex, Group Size and Helping in Three Cities." *Sociometry* 38.2: 180-94.

Plato. 360 B.C. *The Republic.* <http://gutenberg.org/ebooks/150>. Accessed 29 August 2011.

THE HUMAN INSTRUCTION MANUAL

The essays in this section voice a similar concern—the narrowing of the purpose of education down to its most practical, utilitarian (read, economic) aspect. Senior Admissions Counselor Nancy Galindo summarizes it like this: "So many U.S. college students and their families are interested in their undergraduate and graduate education providing an immediate *'Return on Investment.'* I hear some fear and desperation in their inquiry. They don't see how such a return on investment can come from a humanities education. *'Where* will that get me? *What* will that get me?' they question."

Each essay laments that we even have to ask these questions, and offers its own unique answers. Stephen Aizenstat shares, "The study of the humanities is one of the most practical educational orientations I know of. In my mind there's nothing more practical, and nothing that furthers my personal capacity to manage an institution, balance a budget, or work administratively, than to open my relationship to the Muses in art, music, and the humanities. To the extent that I cut myself off from these deeper sources of inspiration is the extent to which I don't perform as effectively in the practical and professional tasks that are asked of me."

Safron Rossi's essay takes up our relationship to the nine Muses of Greek mythology. "The Muses are the framing figures for the collective body of the humanities," she writes. She guides us through each of the Muses, pairing them with a contemporary exemplar who has received their inspiration, illustrating the point that "the grace of the Muses comes to us through art, literature, music, dance, poetry, philosophy, mythology, and depth psychology. Their inspiration opens us into the rhythms of the creative cosmos where we touch upon what is truly human and truly sublime–eternal and temporal." Without this inspiration, she argues, we are living in a wasteland, "a desacralized environment such as ours wherein the humanities and the very areas of their work are considered only in terms of their usefulness or their economic value."

Dara Marks notes in her essay that the arts and humanities are still seen as valuable, especially when they cross over into entertainment. People will pay for that, though they may not pay for *the study of the arts,* may not see the value there. And yet, she writes, "While it is probably true that there is not an overabundance of jobs to be had in fields that emanate directly from humanities courses like art, music, literature, classical languages, and philosophy, can there be any doubt that these courses serve to *humanize* everything else a student studies?" Her essay explores "what the purposeful study of these forms can offer us at its highest level," which, she argues, "is greater consciousness—greater *human* consciousness." In fact, she calls the humanities "the human instruction manual" for how to live. She takes the discipline of the humanities to task, however, for its sometimes haughty elitism, raising the question "If the humanities shelter themselves in such a rarified atmosphere that they hold no seat at the table for the most common among us, then whom do they serve?"

Barbara Mossberg has spent her life in service of the humanities and has often been called upon to defend their value, so we knew from the beginning that we wanted her to contribute an essay to this volume. What we didn't know was at the moment we asked her, she was faced with Rossi's "eternal and temporal," living through the experience of her mother's dying, feeling helpless, floundering, unsure, unmoored. Are the humanities really important, she questions. And then, "I decide to make my criteria for assessing the humanities at the end of the day, how they serve me at this critical life and death moment." Would they serve as Marks' "human instruction manual"? Her discovery: not only are the humanities practical, they are essential, "even when, especially when, life is reduced to the unspeakable, the unspoken, the barely spoken, the hardly heard, the not understood, the not understandable. But because the humanities deal with the essential ways we are human, we may take their usefulness for granted, as a fish considers water."

Mossberg's essay is a perfect one to end on, as her conclusion is one upon which all our essayists would echo. She writes, "In this moment of life and death, and new life, I felt the gift of the humanities as celebrating the human experience in its totality."

Jennifer Leigh Selig

When we split off from the teachings of the great works of art, literature, and music, we split off from thousands of years of human experience and insight. . . . To live in the teachings of the great storytellers, artists, and musicians from all traditions informs our humanity and opens our imagination to ideas and possibilities that would never otherwise be stimulated or experienced.

~Stephen A. Aizenstat

The humanities offer a richness of imagination, and a wealth of creativity that stimulates our inner experience, and it's these experiences that reveal our deepest, most tender, and most authentic knowing.

~Nancy Galindo

Through the arts and the humanities we can touch upon the eternal in the temporal, which means that by hearing the Muses' song we can attend to the education of the whole person. If the Muses are the figures who gracefully frame the humanities as a body of collective wisdom, then let us invoke and honor them in our work. Let us muse on the humanities not as an old or archaic way of having engaged our lives individually and collectively but rather as what founds our human curiosity, passion, and longing for knowledge and wisdom.

~Safron Rossi

Were we to take a more holistic view of the humanities, we might see that language, art, literature, and philosophy conspire to reveal one, essential thing: the human narrative. Encoded in the language of every sonnet and every sitcom, every artistic masterpiece and every mundane mouthful of pop music is a part (no matter how minuscule) of the narrative that forms the human instruction manual. Perhaps, then, the great challenge, the real purpose, of the study of the humanities is to teach us how to read this manual, which consistently reveals that our problems are solvable, our trials are conquerable, and our wounds are healable.

~Dara Marks

I realize that in this demoralized state, I am not alone, and perhaps this knowledge of what we all share, as I consider the usefulness of the humanities, is at the roots of what we need to live. . . . The humanities ensure that on this human journey, we never walk alone.

~**Barbara Mossberg**

WELLSPRINGS OF IMAGINATION, CREATIVITY, AND INNOVATION: AN INTERVIEW WITH DR. STEPHEN AIZENSTAT

Nancy Galindo, PhD

NANCY: What inspires you to have this conversation about humanities education, to write about it, and advocate for it? With your background as a life-long educator in elementary through post-graduate levels, as a clinical psychologist, and as the founding president and Chancellor of Pacifica Graduate Institute, what makes this advocacy so important?

STEVE: Reintroducing humanities education is something I'm passionate about. I think it will allow us to recover the field of education itself. Over the last number of years, perhaps beginning with the "No Child Left Behind" initiative, the emphasis in education has been on accountability, teaching to the test, and implementing uniform assessment instruments, all of which tend to orient around the science of education, as if we could somehow measure students' intelligence, creativity, and talent by how they perform on standardized tests. Most of the assessment instruments are "Scantron" type, which is a system that uses machine-readable papers on which students fill-in a bubble to mark their answers to multiple-choice test questions. Student's test performance is then scored by scanners and ranked by computer software.

We're essentially training kids to read, ingest, and memorize information, and then in some form or fashion, literally regurgitate back what they've ingested. That's so different from the real value of a well-rounded education, in my mind.

NANCY: How would you describe a well-rounded education?

STEVE: A well-rounded education is one that captivates imagination, opens and broadens the student's capacity to become curious, and encourages students to live in the wonderment of what is, not only within the line of the text, but in what exists *between the lines* of text. A well-rounded education invites students to engage with art, whether it's dance, painting, poetry, music, or great literature. These genres do more than convey information, they open our human capacity to create, innovate, and imagine into the future.

In a well-rounded education, there's a place for humanities as well as needed training in the basics. Of course we all need to learn to read and write, and it's essential to have a capacity with numbers as well as an understanding of science. There's no argument on that side of the ledger. Education, however, has been stripped bare of the arts and humanities to such an extent that the kids hardly have an opportunity to read great literature or experience great art, let alone study, savor, and share their insights from these genres. Because of finances and other reasons, most music and art programs have been omitted from the curriculum of K through 12, and even from some undergraduate programs.

NANCY: We're clearly in a trend that emphasizes the basics, and we have a near obsession with standardized testing, but what do you make of the fear and the fact that the U.S. is actually falling behind many of our international competitors in the basics of reading, math, and science?

STEVE: The U.S. is falling behind not because there aren't enough classes in those subjects, but arguably because the imaginative and creative desires that fuel the excitement of learning, and the capacity to master these fields, has been dimmed and diminished.

I'll give you an example. Not too long ago, I went to a regional meeting of presidents in higher education. It included a panel of CEOs from multinational corporations. The CEO's addressed the presidents and offered what they thought would best serve our students in today's world, in this era, and at this time. The educators anticipated the obvious, that the CEOs would advocate for more training in math, science, and logic. We were convinced this would be their message.

We listened in shock and surprise when the corporate CEOs said that what's missing in today's education, from K through 12 to the graduate level, is the cultivation of imagination and innovation that comes with studying the humanities! *Plus*, they asked us to do what we could to develop our students' ability to have productive and collaborative relationships, a well-rounded life, and a fulfilling inner life.

NANCY: I wouldn't expect them to say that? How did they come to that?

STEVE: They said: If you can give us whole human beings at the end of their formal education, then we can take a few months to train them in the latest technology and specialization of their craft. They added, parenthetically, that by the time students completed their education, most of the technology and systems they've mastered will already be outdated. It would be best, they said, for corporations and employers to do the technical postgraduate training; and it would be best for educators to foster and train *whole, imaginative, and creative human beings.*

These qualities are being lost, they said. We may lose our competitive edge in the world marketplace because the school systems are no longer vigorously and wholeheartedly supporting students in their innovative, imaginative, and creative lives. This is the sort of people we need in today's world, not more narrow-minded, highly disciplined, specialists.

NANCY: You know it's paradoxical because I've also heard international scholars, commentators, and historians point to what the U.S. has always had going for it characteristically, and that's our imaginative, inventive, and experimental edge.

STEVE: They're referring to the American Dream. Historically, our country has been a place of great innovation. America has always been regarded as an enormous source of new ideas and the capacity to dream the world forward.

Now the opposite is true. We've had such a swing to the fantasy that good education equals particularized, standardized, learning objectives, and uniform assessment and evaluation. We've lost the creativity in the curriculum and the classroom, and this is what would support the very thing we've been noted for through the centuries, which is to do what's innovative and inventive. It's what has lived so long at the root of our national character.

NANCY: Let me offer another concern. In my work at Pacifica Graduate Institute, I counsel prospective students who are interested in applying to Ph.D. programs in depth psychology and mythological studies. They tell me about their struggle between their love of studying of myth, humanities, and psychology, and the push to follow what they call a "practical" educational path. They're concerned about preparing themselves for a particular job title and the highest earning potential. They wonder if they have to give up one for the other. Their families express concern about the "practicality" of their education as well.

STEVE: The study of the humanities is one of the most practical educational orientations I know of. In my mind there's nothing more practical, and nothing that furthers my personal capacity to manage an institution, balance a budget, or work administratively, than to open my relationship to the Muses in art, music, and the humanities. To the extent that I cut myself off from these deeper sources of inspiration is the extent to which I don't perform as effectively in the practical and professional tasks that are asked of me, and asked in any career.

Frankly, I could be a better plumber, electrician, accountant, school administrator, or car mechanic as a result of having a rich and deeply felt imaginative life. In my work as the chancellor of a graduate institute, I know that I'm more innovative, curious, motivated, and happier to be alive when I'm connected to the creative life force that informs my capabilities and capacities.

NANCY: The humanities are "life-giving" as they support us in our ability to carry out the practical day-to-day tasks in our profession and in our life.

STEVE: Yes. I'll tell you an interesting story about this. Recently, I had the privilege of meeting with a group of Chinese educators. They had invited an elite panel of American educators to their country and asked the Americans to share their best new practices in education. The Americans were so proud to offer what was going on in their new initiatives with standardized learning objectives, assessment-based teaching, and testing.

The Chinese, of course, listened intently, patiently, and with great respect for what the Americans were saying, only to offer afterwards: "How curious? That's what we were doing 15 years ago."

The Americans were astounded, having thought stereotypically that the Chinese would be similarly regulated, uniform, and precise. Just the opposite was true. The Chinese discovered that reintroducing the arts and humanities in early education encouraged inventive thinking and the capacity to be creative. They're seeing the result. It's the Chinese students, not the students graduating from American universities that have the competitive edge in the global marketplace.

NANCY: We've switched places with one another.

STEVE: Yes, we've switched. Education in China now looks like what the U.S. education looked like 15 or 20 years ago. They have classes in music. We don't. They have classes in the creative arts. Woodshop! Remember woodshop? That's a relic of the past. And dance, dance is now offered less frequently in the American system, but dance is vivid, alive, supported, and funded in the Chinese system of education.

NANCY: It's surprising.

STEVE: Yes!

NANCY: Let me offer another vexing question regarding the humanities. So many U.S. college students and their families are interested in their undergraduate and graduate education providing an immediate *"Return on Investment."* I hear some fear and desperation in their inquiry. They don't see how such a return on investment can come from a humanities education. *"Where* will that get me? *What* will that get me?" they question.

STEVE: I think, out of necessity in today's world, people are looking at education's return on investment. This is in service to getting a good job, paying back student loans, and developing the means to support themselves. Folks want to buy a house. They need enough money to raise a family. They want to determine whether their education will give them what they need in order to accomplish these goals and succeed in the world financially. The current economic crises have created this sort of fear and desperation.

There needs to be a training component in education so that people have the capacity to go into the marketplace and find work that's not only of value to them personally, but will also pay the bills.

NANCY: Of course who they are also affects their success. So many qualities are important, not only what marketable skills they have, but how relational they are, how generous, how interesting, how interested, and how inspired and creative they are. The humanities help shape who a person is.

STEVE: True, and additionally, in terms of the technology that's needed, when information is taught in such a way that all one is asked to do is memorize skill sets or facts, it leaves out the *inspiration that lives behind the technology*. When we're teaching to standardized tests in math, English, and science, with a nineteenth century point of view, we have to remember that there's hardly a U.S. manufacturing sector left for people to fit into, or find jobs in.

What's needed is an innovative point of view that will create new technologies and new opportunities that are inventive and innovative. Students will have to cultivate a career based on what's actual in today's world and what will anticipate the future.

NANCY: We're living in a time when creativity and innovation have taken on a more vital necessity because of the environmental, economic, and cultural crises we're experiencing.

STEVE: Yes. What's actual in today's world are jobs in which people need to develop inspiration and innovation as they move along. Remember how people flocked to the movie to watch how Facebook was created? That story and those images are so fascinating because this sort of inspiration is what the marketplace and the world place are asking from us now. We need innovations that are developed outside the box and *birthed out of the new*.

The way to get into the new job market is to open and support the generativity that's inherent in each of us. That only happens when we're engaged in our creative process, and *creativity's wellspring is the humanities*.

NANCY: If you were to describe how the humanities infuse creativity, and how it in turn enhances our professional skills, how would you describe it?

STEVE: Well, I'll speak a bit about my own professional experience here at Pacifica Graduate Institute. Pacifica began as a school whose primary discipline was psychology; and psychology is a craft and science that includes how to be effective in creating a diagnosis, how to assess a person's behavior, and how to determine what kind of treatment or medicines will be constructive. Psychologists and therapists are trained in the science of psychology and this is all to the good. It's required for an effective and ethical practice.

However, Pacifica also grew out of the conviction that in addition to science, there is more that's essential to the study and practice of psychology. Depth psychological traditions which are taught at Pacifica, are also rooted

134

in myth, literature, poetry, and the arts. We include dream, imagination, culture, nature, and more. The humanities infuse psychology with more than skill sets. The humanities offer psychologists the capacity to anchor into the depth of human experience, and as a result, be more effective with their clients, in their communities, with everyone they're related to, and with themselves.

When psychologists work in communities that are suffering gang violence, joblessness, or addictions such as alcohol or drugs, and they only know how to give topical answers or offer skill-sets, they miss the cultural and psychological underpinnings of what's gone awry to begin with.

NANCY: A psychologist who's educated in the humanities could listen into the imaginal realities and archetypal stories that are living below the surface and influencing the current difficulty or desperation in the community.

STEVE: Yes. There's something important beneath the surface that needs attention, and the way to get underneath the surface of a symptom or illness, or a condition in the community, is to reveal the depth of soul that's being expressed. The way to move into that depth, is to anchor into a broader, more creative, and more open psychological mind, heart, and soul.

When we split off from the teachings of the great works of art, literature, and music, we split off from thousands of years of human experience and insight.

NANCY: The humanities are anchored in ancient wisdom.

STEVE: Yes, that's what compels us to read and experience what's alive and active in the great myths, regardless of whether they're rooted in Greece, Africa, or the far reaches of Asia. To learn how indigenous peoples throughout time have understood the patterns that permeate human behavior is to learn a depth and breadth of cultural wisdom that's invaluable.

Native American myths and stories are rich with wisdom. They offer us a capacity to hear the world as alive, and not dead. They offer what it means to live in a world where nature is valued. They hold the world of things, creatures, and landscapes as a world that ought not be disposed of, or exploited, but deeply valued and appreciated for the spirit and soul that's alive in all things.

NANCY: When the humanities offer such richness, they open our capacity to imagine and innovate with a more humane wisdom and a greater sensitivity to nature.

STEVE: Yes, the humanities open us to the natural world. Being in touch with our imaginative potential opens our sensitivity and sensate awareness to the world we live in, to the landscapes, mountains, seas, and rivers. Nature becomes animated and alive for us. Our relationship with nature informs human nature and our life and work are immensely enriched.

NANCY: It seems such a loss then, to remove the humanities from education.

STEVE: I'll tell you a story that's relevant. I was in a high school classroom a number of months ago and I met a most extraordinary English teacher. She was in her late fifties, a career teacher, the best the high school had to offer. She had spent her career teaching two groups of students, those who were having a hard time in the classroom, and those who were top students, the ones who were going make it into Ivy League schools and the top universities around the country.

This woman had spent 30 years collecting the great stories and teaching the works of literature that she felt were incredibly exciting and relevant for the student's 15, 16, and 17-year-old lives. These were stories that would guide the students as they matured and moved on.

Five years ago, when the standardized testing movement really got going, and the school district was dependent on funding as a result of student's score, all her files and lesson plans, along with those great novels and pieces of literature, had to be stored in the back room. You know what she spent the following years doing? She taught kids how to increase their test scores and their SATs, including in the literature component. She coached students to achieve the high test scores they needed to get into the best colleges and universities.

NANCY: How did she feel about that? How did she respond to it?

STEVE: When I went to visit her classroom and meet with her personally, she was in grief. All that work, and all those extraordinary stories and resources, were missing. They were locked away in a cabinet in the back room and the kids didn't even have a shot at engaging the depth of the extraordinary literature she had collected.

In years past she would have the kids reading those great stories. Of course there would be tests, but the tests wouldn't be answers to standardized multiple-choice questions, they'd be expressive essays. Evaluation would also be based on interactive activity between the kids. They'd be collaborating on art projects, staging plays, and making movies. They'd be discussing the themes they were studying and exploring how these themes were applicable in their lives, and in their way of being in the world. The kids would be imagining what their contribution in the world would be. They'd be having lively discussions about existential questions and they'd be thinking philosophically, psychologically, and outside the box.

This great teacher was deeply saddened by the dominance of the standardized tests and assessments, and the consequences of this. Yet, what do today's parents want? Parents want their kid's test scores to be high enough to get into the best schools. Of course they do. And the school district needs the funding. Of course it does. However, when education is based on standardized achievement that's measured by test scores alone, and at the expense of the humanities, imagination, and depth of experience, there are incredible consequences.

NANCY: What can we do to mitigate the consequences then? How can educators reawaken the imaginative and creative impulses in their students? How can one go about that?

STEVE: One can go about it by offering students opportunities to interact with one another and with the possibilities the curriculum opens. The teacher can ask what creative insights the particular text or subject inspires, whether it's a problem in mathematics, the business of doing business, or the effective practice of science, it's how the educator and students come to the subject and interact with it that's the key.

Add the humanities: go to the opera, listen to music, watch professional dance, read *The Great Gatsby*, *Moby-Dick*, and the Greek myths. To live in the teachings of the great storytellers, artists, and musicians from all traditions informs our humanity and opens our imagination to ideas and possibilities that would never otherwise be stimulated or experienced.

NANCY: Where are the esteemed and authoritative voices for the reinstatement of humanities education?

STEVE: I'm reminded of Gregory Bateson, the extraordinary thinker and theoretical scientist. Not long before his death, he wrote a memorandum to his fellow Regents of the University of California. Included in his book, *Mind and Nature* (1979), this statement offers his plea, that as educators, we need to teach not only contents, but teach our students how to shift contexts. In addition to the many distinguished things he did in his life, he was a Regent, and he wrote: "At the end of my life, my plea to you is that when you think about education, teach not only contents, but teach your students how to shift contexts."

He went on to offer that, in the emerging world, young people need to know how to embrace the notion of paradox and contradiction, the seeming impossibility of it all. He said that teaching to the rational mind alone, or exclusively focusing on linear thought, would cripple the next generation as they came face to face with a postmodern world, a world of contradictions, paradoxical ideas, and intents.

Bateson also spoke about the importance of imagination, offering that cultivating imagination, rather than teaching only information, would open a student's ability to be forward thinking and hold a multiplicity of ideas. He said that imagination would help students navigate the shifts in context that first appear to be impossible and allow them to innovate.

NANCY: It's not by chance then, that when we're speaking about humanities education, we keep coming back to imagination.

STEVE: Imagination is anchored in the humanities because they ask us to imagine into life. They invite us to be responsive to the world through an aesthetic way of being, rather an object-driven, competitive, or money-driven way of being.

Einstein said that "imagination is more important than knowledge," that "knowledge is limited," while "imagination circles the world." This is the kind of education we need. You know Einstein was dyslexic; he had trouble adding numbers, yet in imagination he was able to see the great picture and work through the paradoxes that presented themselves. The world is filled with stories of those who, for whatever reason, have difficulty with particular skills but have access to an imaginative and creative mind.

NANCY: Then it follows that we can't teach, treat, or test students in the same "standardized" way.

STEVE: Yes, in fact, when you go into a classroom today there are about 20 percent of students who will do very well and get the right answers to the questions posed by the Scantron-style testing. They'll do great. They'll get high achievement scores on their SATs and GREs, and so forth. Their intelligence is well-suited to this kind of measurement. They have an intelligence that flourishes with rational and linear thought.

When you look at the other 80 percent of students, you get curious about what intelligence it is that they're gifted with; and then you see that it's emotional intelligence, and imaginative and intuitive intelligence that grows, not out of linear thinking, but out of the creative process itself.

NANCY: You remind me of another story that Einstein tells about how he developed the theory of relativity. He imagined himself running alongside a light beam! He was so curious what the light would look like. He always began and carried forward with imagination.

STEVE: Yes, extraordinary creative capacities begin and carry on in imagination.

NANCY: And with passionate curiosity.

STEVE: Exactly. Imagination opens people to their innate curiosity. What's so extraordinary about curiosity is that it has a force of its own. It has an instinctual root. To follow one's curiosity is to follow a different kind of intelligence that takes us to places we'd never otherwise discover and experience.

NANCY: You also have deep appreciation for dream life. "Dream Tending" is the subject of your passionate research and close to your heart and soul. What does dream life offer to the humanities and the development of creativity, innovation, and imagination?

STEVE: If we go back to Bateson's encouragement to ponder contexts, we realize we have the ability to move off the page and explore other realms, those of imagination, perception, and dreaming. Innumerable new ideas, perceptions, and innovations first come in dream. When we go to sleep at night and our eyes are closed, something else comes awake. We can make the case that what comes awake in dream, are the humanities themselves, because dreams bring extraordinary stories, fascinating figures, living images, and landscapes from all ages.

The stories of our species and the archetypes of the collective human experience are revealed in dreams. I would urge us to have the courage to consider dreams as legitimate and credible curriculum. We need to encourage students to "talk dream" and "talk story" with one another. This is one of the richest sources of discovering new contexts and new ways of being.

Dreams and the humanities not only expand our awareness of who we are, they give us a sense of deep belonging. They situate us in story, relationship, and the place of being. We see ourselves not only as persons who are heroically trying to do valuable work and make meaning out of the events of our life, we experience ourselves belonging to something bigger. Dreams and humanities offer a context, a purpose, and a sense of belonging to something larger and deeper that informs our life and our way of being in the world.

NANCY: We discover expansive experiences and deep metaphorical intelligence in dreams and the humanities.

STEVE: Yes, I think that's what Gregory Bateson was emphasizing when he was talking about living in paradox and the importance of understanding metaphor. Dream and story take us from one context to another, they teach us to think symbolically, and they allow us to notice that things aren't necessarily the way they appear to be on the surface, but may be inviting us into a deeper experience or possibility for the future.

NANCY: I'm reminded of something that Carl Jung said: that we learn most profoundly from what's revealed in dream, imagination, and inner experience, not from what is told or taught to us. It's our inner experience that creates the lasting impression.

STEVE: I couldn't agree more. In this day and age, we're exposed to so much information, it's extraordinary; and we often take too few occasions to listen to dream, imagination, and inner experience.

In all my years of teaching K through 12, at the community college level, and at the graduate and post graduate level, the one thing that I've learned that has forever stayed constant, is that as useful as information is, as extraordinary as the content of my lecture might be or not be, what people actually take home with them is an experience. Their experience is a result of being touched by something that's been offered or shared, by engaging the material with another person, and by listening in to their own experience.

NANCY: The humanities offer a richness of imagination, and a wealth of creativity that stimulates our inner experiences; and it's these experiences that reveal our deepest, most tender, and most authentic knowing.

STEVE: Yes, the humanities originate in human experience and *give back* to human experience. They open what may have been dormant in us for a long time, and they amplify and animate what's most alive in us. They move us more deeply into inner life and inspire what's yet to be revealed. Eros is sparked and given time to incubate and unfold, allowing us to give expression to the soulfulness and depth of experience it offers. Our very humanity is rekindled and awakened by a certain passage, a poem, a piece of music, a great idea, or an experience of beauty. This is the extraordinary contribution of humanities education.

MUSING ON THE HUMANITIES

Safron Rossi, Ph.D

Daughters of Mnemosyne and thundering Zeus,
Pierian Muses, renowned, illustrious,
many-shaped and beloved of the mortals you visit.
You give birth to unblemished virtue in every discipline,
you nourish the soul and set thought aright,
as you become leaders and mistresses of the mind's power.
—Athanassakis, *The Orphic Hymns*, 76

In Joseph Campbell's essay "The Mystery Number of the Goddess" (2007), the roots and later manifestations of the female divine are explored through various cultures, mythologies and images. Of particular interest to my thoughts on the importance of the humanities is a beautiful illustration titled "The Music of the Spheres" created in 1496 by a Florentine named Gafurius. This symbolically rich drawing shows the Goddesses' presence in the Italian Renaissance in the form of the nine Muses: Thalia (bucolic poetry), Clio (history), Calliope (epic poetry), Terpischore (dance), Melpomene (tragedy), Eratho (erotic poetry), Euterpe (music), Polyhymnia (sacred poetry), and Urania (astronomy). This drawing reveals how the Muses, the Greek Goddesses of music, poetry and the arts, inspire the nine main areas of human knowledge, the humanities, and their relationship to the cosmos. This is the cosmos of our imagination, our history, how we find ourselves in relation to other times, other people, other ideas. The Muses are the framing figures for the collective body of the humanities.

Today many of us feel as if we are living in a desacralized environment when we are disconnected from the *here and now* where the wisdom of the past is embodied consciously in the present, or to say it another way, where the eternal is experienced in the temporal. We are in a wasteland when access to the Muses is controlled, limited, and accessible only by the select few. Campbell compares this tension to William Blake's poetic works wherein he sought to revision humankind's relationship to Yahweh and his avenging angels. Allow us into the garden of paradise, Blake said, so that we may taste from the trees of knowledge and wisdom. Let us touch the eternal in the temporal. I believe that it is the humanities that allow us to connect to the *here and now* and experience the eternal in the temporal. It was poetry for Sappho and William Blake, myth for C. G. Jung and Joseph Campbell, music for Wolfgang Mozart and Loreena McKennitt, philosophy for Socrates and Hélène Cixous. The grace of the Muses comes to us through art, literature, music, dance, poetry, philosophy, mythology, and depth psychology. Their inspiration opens us into the rhythms of the creative cosmos where we touch upon what is truly human and truly sublime—eternal and temporal.

The passage is not easy these days; there are difficulties and challenges one must overcome in order to be able to hear the Muses' song. The guardians of the path to the Muses are fierce and Gafurius' drawing reveals that it is none other than a kin to Cerberus, a beast with the head of a lion, a wolf and a dog. Campbell says that this beast is Devouring Time in its three aspects of past, present and future, the temporal through which the eternal is ever present and experienced on earth (2007, 145). Edgar Wind illustrates the connection between the beasts and time thus, "The lion, violent and sudden expresses the present; she-wolf, which drags away its victims is the image of the past, robbing us of memories; the dog, fawning on its master, suggests to us the future which ceaselessly beguiles us with hope." (1968, 259) These are the beasts that Dante encounters just prior to entering with the poet Virgil into the Inferno: the lion of pride, the leopard of desire and the she-wolf of fear and violence. They belong in the same company as Mara (fear) and Kama (desire), who visited Buddha so to tempt him out from his meditative transcendence.

The same three-headed beast challenges the humanities in our culture today. The lion is the current dehumanizing of the disciplines that constitute the humanities in favor of departments and fields of study that are focused on economics, job acquisition, and "hard" science. This is the sudden and violent expression of our collective educational values at this moment. The she-wolf is robbing us of our memories of the majesty and importance of the humanities as a body of knowledge that allows us to engage, human-to-human, in our world. If we lose the humanities we lose our memory of the fact that it is precisely the humanities that have been the educational substratum of all the individuals who have achieved greatness for humanity. These include the founders of our country, individuals who have worked for political ideals and reform, social justice, scientific and medical advancements, works of artistic beauty and depth that transcend time. Lastly, we are in the thrall of the dog that beguiles us with hope for the future, the molding of the youth through an education that is based on usefulness, practicality, generalized norms and economic currency rather than on the pillars of human knowledge that never decrease in value. The humanities are the gold bullion that money no longer measures its value against. Whether we are on the cutting edge of solar panel production and technological advancements in engineering, if we can only speak one language we will not be able to communicate with the rest of the world. If we cannot see that the structures of our Western political, social and cultural establishments are based on ancient models, ideals and myths, we are lost in a condition of rootlessness. If we cannot learn to read a poem and feel the aching beauty of a fleeting moment that was captured in a few lines, then we succumb to a state of dead usefulness, like automatons, machines.

We cannot abide such a wasteland. Anyone who connects to the eternal through the forms of the temporal—artists, scholars, poets, painters, dancers, historians, philosophers, and writers—cannot exist in a desacralized environment such as ours wherein the humanities and the very areas of their work are considered only in terms of their usefulness or their economic value. The wasteland is transformed by surrendering to the *here and now*, putting our head in the lion's mouth and surrendering to this moment so that we can hear the Muses. Immediately with our recognition of the *here and now*, "the hidden Muse, Surda Thalia, wakes. Her voice is heard. What until then had been the nocturnal silence of a wasteland of dust and toil becomes eloquent of a universal joy" (Campbell 2007, 150). The Muses and their cosmos which represent the humanities and the knowledge of those arts opens up before and within us.

Sing to us Muses of the glory and power of the humanities.

The wasteland spreads and encroaches upon land that strives to attend to the soil and roots of our collective history and our attempts to sow the seed and bear the fruit of the arts and the humanities. Yet the Muses' song *can* be heard. I was taught how to hear their whispers which became songs, taught how to praise their gifts by following the threads of their gowns through books and art. My experience as a student at Hampshire College, a small liberal arts school in Western Massachusetts, taught me how to follow the chord of inspiration, how to discern and weave science with art, literature with image, social theory with the literary fabric of culture. My graduate education at Pacifica Graduate Institute deepened the legacy of philosophy, literature, mythology, depth psychology and cultural studies so to see the metaphoric within the concrete, to read cultural and personal crises from the symbolic and mythic lenses. This means that I have been taught how to seek connections, differentiate images and narratives, read through headlines and into political or intellectual debates and see what is at work below, as well as what ideas, needs, histories are at play.

On one level it is exceedingly difficult to imagine defending the humanities at all, so central are they to the health, life and quality of our culture. It is incomprehensible to me that the value of learning another language, learning how to read critically, how to find and hear the echoes of the *Divine Comedy* in *Moby-Dick*, under attack by indifference. Yet it appears that this is where we find ourselves, what the educational councils with their funding apparatuses have crossed off the lists. We must place our head in the lion's mouth and hear Thalia attune us through her song to the other Muses. Then we can see all the ways that the arts, poetry, literature, philosophy, letters, are kept alive right now and where they continue to inspire in spite of the voices that prevaricate and tempt us to look, listen, elsewhere.

I will share with you where I see the Muses' grace in our world through the hands and heart of the artists and scholars whose arts are necessary to the fabric of our experience, core to the traditions we need to care and attend to, feed and nourish, with all our might. By looking at the contemporary work that illuminates each Muse, her vibrant symbolic body is enlivened, and so too the development of the whole person through their arts. We shall begin with Thalia for Campbell says it is she who is the "opening of any artist's sense to knowledge of the universal body of which his [*sic*] own is a part" (2007, 150).

THALIA—"BLOOMING AND ABUNDANCE"
Muse of Bucolic Poetry

Thalia inspires the poetry and songs in praise of the blossoming innocence of a living earth. Walking alongside Emerson and Whitman, Pulitzer Prize winning poet Mary Oliver is a contemporary voice in the tradition of romantic nature poetry. In her poem "Wild Geese" (1986), she invites us to open our eyes to our place among all things on earth. Through the deserts of our sorrows, among the trees in our silence, in the call of the wild geese flying above, we can find ourselves in the *here and now*. We need only open ourselves up to Nature's song—Thalia's grace—heard in the voice of another creature, the wind in the branches, as well as the patterns etched in sand dunes.

CLIO—"ACCLAIM"
Muse of History and Writing

Women's voices have risen in both individual and collective song these last hundred years to reveal a whole other expression of selfhood. Our understanding of history has been radically altered once women were free to articulate their perspectives, voice their critiques and share their imaginings. Hélène Cixous, French third wave feminist writer, poet and playwright, speaks of an "ecriture feminine," woman's writing that comes from the female body, a writing that has its own language because it is embodied and articulated by women.

Clio, muse of history and writing, inspires by giving wings and courage to women who seek an equal and yet different expression of self rooted in the female body and the female psyche. The French feminists' *voler* means they fly and steal. Through flying over the terrain of patrifocal history and patriarchal fantasy wherein the male experience is the rule against which all is measured and valued, we are able to gain a new perspective and thus navigate the terrain of language and history, apprehend its blockages, deconstruct its limits, and then steal what we need in order to recover our own history, write our translations of meaning, as well as imagine and articulate our symbolic references. As we come to our own female voices, we trade the rigid forms that have dictated the images of what is female or feminine for something more supple. History, language, literature, the arts, psychology, all slip and slide in their meaning in this act of *voler* and the embodied feminine speaks, writes and imagines herself forward.

CALLIOPE—"OF THE BEAUTIFUL VOICE"
Muse of Epic Poetry and Eloquence in Speech

The epics of antiquity are told and retold because they express truths of experience that are valid through time. They reveal the archetypal patterns and figures that give form and figure to the common threads of human experience. Themes such as life after the loss of love, the descent into the underworld and the heroic journey are present not only in the great epics of the past but in the stories that we tell and live today.

For instance, Calliope enchanted the Coen brothers who wrote the film *O Brother Where Art Thou,* a retelling of Homer's epic poem *The Odyssey,* set in the Deep South during the 1930's. Herein the great theme of the journey home, the yearning for return was revitalized, through humor, song and tragedy. In a similar way, Margaret Atwood's *Penelopiad* gave Penelope, Odysseus' patient and cunning wife, a voice by which she wove her own memories, experiences and feelings into the ageless tapestry called epic.

TERPISCHORE—"SHE WHO ENJOYS DANCING"
Muse of Dance and All Creative Movement

The devastating Cartesian split between mind and body is being healed. The voice of the body and its connection to psyche and nature has become a focus in various fields including psychology, education, spirituality, and medicine. In depth psychology Marion Woodman stands as one of the pioneers weaving together body movement, dance, and drama as vehicles for the embodied soul's voice to be heard. She writes that the body "makes the soul visible and soul conflicts become body conflicts" (1993, 153) Woodman, one of the first Jungian analysts to work and write about eating disorders, believes that their symptoms and issues are messages from the unconscious delivered metaphorically through the body. Therefore bridging our conscious understanding with the soul knowledge that is expressed through the body can bring about profound healing. In the passionate and intense patience devoted to bodies voice what is revealed is presence—the presence of the self, the presence of soul, the *here and now*. If dance is archetypal imagery, as Woodman (152) says, then in dancing what we see is the soul in action. Our bodies are one of the instruments of psyche and can radically heal when given freedom and room to dance.

MELPOMENE—"THE SINGER"
Muse of Tragedy

Tragedy and the heart's purifying and compassionate opening have long been companions. The ancient Greeks understood that catharsis, the emotional cleansing of the heart, was necessary for the soul and it could be ritually activated through the genre of tragedy. Collective witnessing is an important aspect of Melpomene's art, represented by the figures of the tragic chorus as well as the audience. I see the threads between tragedy, compassion and collective witnessing growing stronger in our world today by individuals who have risen onto the world platform in order to tell their people's stories which are often tragic and yet suffused with spiritual and humanitarian yearnings which open upon the heart.

The Dalai Lama speaks of the loss of his people's spiritual land and home to inspire compassion not only in collective consciousness but also in practice. The 2011 Nobel Peace Prize was awarded jointly to Ellen Johnson Sirleaf, Leymah Gbowee and Tawakkul Karman "for their non-violent struggle for the safety of women and for women's rights to full participation in peace-building work" (Nobelprize.org 2011).

Collectively witnessing and continuing to educate cultural, historical and spiritual fluency is necessary to open our hearts; the humanities serves as the genesis of this opening.

ERATHO—"AWAKENER OF DESIRE"
Muse of Erotic and Lyric Poetry

The "Sisters of Mercy," who are none other than the Muses, saved Leonard Cohen. Listen to the song and you will understand. A voice of desire and longing, Cohen has the poet's silver darting tongue while his lyrics evoke the softness of love's body, the mystery of union, and the inevitably of separation. By way of his song titles I offer a poem:

Take This Waltz
If It Be Your Will
Dance Me to the End of Love
I Tried To Leave You
Why Don't You Try
Lover Lover Lover
Take This Longing
Hallelujah
I'm Your Man
Ain't No Cure For Love
Leaving Green Sleeves
Coming Back To You

Eratho can loosen our limbs with a glance because the erotic is the power that compels us towards becoming an *I* through the desire for a *Thou*. Let us pray along with her laurelled poet and ask her to take this longing from our tongues so that image and voice may be given to our ancient yearnings.

EUTERPE—"GIVER OF JOY"
Muse of Music

It is nearly an indescribable joy when the rhythm and lyrics of a song or album gives body and voice to what you feel is true. This is Euterpe's joy. In *The Suburbs* (2011), an album by Canadian indie rock band Arcade Fire, the songs circle around the damage inflicted by suburban wastelands, the hardness of the youth, and the asphyxiation of shopping-mall oriented lives. "*The Suburbs* burns on behalf of the belief that modern culture is missing its heart—and to give up the search is to send one's soul to oblivion" (Marchese n.d.). Arcade Fire's music has an easy grace because it breathes and stretches through lyrics that, with a righteous clarity, define the issues of our modern lives.

Caught up in the worship of idols and in the desperation of a crumbling culture, their song "Rococo" shows how modern kids are "using big words that they don't understand" and that "they seem so wild but they're so tame." The album's hard rhythms and cutting lyrics evoke the disconnect between the surface images we are sold and our feeling deep within that something isn't right. This is most provocatively expressed in the song "Modern Man" where we hear echoed back to us the belief that we are "the chosen few" but we are wasted, "if you feel so right how come you can't sleep at night?" Their music challenges us to experience in rhythmic clarity what is happening in our world.

POLYHYMNIA—"SHE OF MANY HYMNS"
Muse of Sacred Poetry, Song and Storytelling

C. G. Jung argued that it is critical to our psychological health to know what myth we are living. James Hillman furthers Jung's belief when he suggested, "Psychology shows myths in modern dress and myths show our depth psychology in ancient dress" (1995, 90). The connection between mythology and psychology, as the two above quotes reveal, is vital and so it has become one of the central concerns of depth psychology to keep the myths from all cultures and religious traditions alive. Myth and the art of storytelling in depth psychology therefore take the first seat, the one closest to the hearth fire.

Polyhymnia's presence is nearer still when we regard depth psychology as a polytheistic psychology, one that honors all of the gods. The multiplicity of figures and the polyvalence of psyche and myth are attended, questioned, reflected upon in the service of soul-making. The gods never come alone and so soul-making requires Polyhymnia, the muse of many songs, many voices.

URANIA—"THE CELESTIAL ONE"
Muse of Astronomy and Metaphysics

The study of the heavens, planets and stars has been a preoccupation of humankind for millennia. The science of astronomy and the art of astrology, once understood to be identical, both turn to Urania the Celestial One for vision and knowledge in the peaceful solitude of the night sky.

Archetypal astrology, deeply influenced by the traditions of the Neo-Platonic writers, philosophers and artists in the Renaissance, as well as C.G. Jung and James Hillman's work, returns us to the deep interconnectedness of the cosmos and the human soul. In his book *Cosmos and Psyche: Intimations of a New World View*, Richard Tarnas turns to the premise of the *anima mundi*, the ensouled world, a vision that draws upon the spiritual, philosophic and artistic understandings that all of life is connected, and that the world is itself ensouled. The heavens, earth and all animate beings are in a relationship of meaningful correspondence, suffused by the archetypal energies that structure our universe.

CONCLUSION
I would like to return to Gafurius' drawing the "Music of the Spheres" and its illustration of the celestial cosmos of our imagination via the art and form of the Muses. Through the arts and the humanities we can touch upon the eternal in the temporal, which means that by hearing the Muses' song we can attend to the education of the whole person. If the Muses are the figures who gracefully frame the humanities as a body of collective wisdom, then let us invoke and honor them in our work. Let us muse on the humanities not as an old or archaic way of having engaged our lives individually and collectively but rather as what founds our human curiosity, passion, and longing for knowledge and wisdom.

REFERENCES
Arcade Fire. 2010. *The Suburbs*. Merge. CD.

Athanassakis, Apostolos. 1977. *The Orphic Hymns: Text, Translation, and Notes*. Missoula: Scholars Press.

Campbell, Joseph. 2007. "The Mystery Number of the Goddess." *The Mythic Dimension: Selected Essays, 1959–1987*. Ed. Antony Van Couvering. Novato, CA: New World Library. 92-150

Hillman, James. 1995. *Oedipus Variations*. Woodstock, CT: Spring Publications.

Marchese, David. N.d. "Review: Arcade Fire, The Suburbs."
<http://www.spin.com/reviews/arcade-fire-suburbs-merge>. Accessed 18
December 2011.

Nobelprize.org. 2011. "The Nobel Peace Prize 2011".
<http://www.nobelprize.org/nobel_prizes/peace/laureates/2011/>. Accessed 26
October 2011.

Oliver, Mary. 1986. "Wild Geese." *Dream Work*. New York: Atlantic Monthly Press.

Wind, Edgar. 1968. *Pagan Mysteries in the Renaissance*. New York: W. W. Norton.

Woodman, Marion. 1993. *Conscious Femininity*. Toronto, Canada: Inner City Books.

THE HUMANITIES:
TO BE, OR NOT TO BE

Dara Marks

People travel to wonder . . . at the height of the mountains, at the huge waves of the sea, at the long courses of rivers, at the vast compass of the ocean, at the circular motion of the stars, and they pass themselves by without wondering.
~St. Augustine, *AD 354–430*

The primary difficulty in writing a defense of the Humanities is that no one is really against them—entirely. Everyone loves some type of art, especially in the form of entertainment. And, few people are completely disinclined to pay for the arts, especially in the form of entertainment. It's paying for *the study of the arts* that seems to be the rub. But, even here, the argument is seldom made that the humanities are of no value. It's just that in terms of "bang for the buck," humanities classes are often considered of less value than courses of study that can actually get someone a job; or so the line of reasoning goes.

Of course, the other side of the argument can be equally as strident. What good is an auto engineer or a computer programmer who has only learned what is already common knowledge in that field? In order to design and develop the next new thing, one must be able to creatively intuit or at least be sensitive to the needs of the consumer. So, how does one develop this sensitivity? It should seem obvious that the best approach would be to study our humanness, our humanity.

While it is probably true that there is not an overabundance of jobs to be had in fields that emanate directly from humanities courses like art, music, literature, classical languages, and philosophy, can there be any doubt that these courses serve to *humanize* everything else a student studies?

However, having said this, I must also (regrettably) add, *so what?* Humanities courses *are* closing. That's simply a fact. Rail against this injustice as we might, the terrible truth is that we wouldn't be having this discussion if the specter of obsolescence weren't looming. Obsolescence occurs when something is no longer *wanted*, whether or not it is still considered viable.

Nothing in nature thrives simply because it should. On this point Darwin cautioned us that it isn't necessarily the strongest or the most intelligent that survives, it is the one who is the most adaptable to change. Though it has its roots in Greek antiquity, the humanities we study today are in many ways a vestige of the Renaissance movement that spanned the 14th to 17th centuries, enhanced by the Enlightenment of the 18th century. So, perhaps, it *is* time for an update.

Half a millennium ago we were just coming to terms with the idea that, factually, the Earth is round. Today, we're on the cusp of embracing its metaphorical "flatness." Boundaries are falling away, opening potential pathways of interconnectedness that heretofore could never have been imagined. Whereas the philosophical leanings of the past took us down the road labeled "You're not the king of me!" today's philosophers point us toward an even greater horizon where one day, hopefully, as that great philosopher John Lennon foresaw, "the world will live as one" (Lennon, *Imagine*).

Fine art, literature, music, and dance are also experiencing an epic shift of consciousness. Once art was predominately the province of the affluent and cultural elite; now it is no longer a rarified experience. Modern technologies allow everyone to acquire all forms of speech, movement, music, and imagery on demand—the good, the bad, and the ugly. In fact, we're not just privy to it, we're bombarded by it.

Access to the arts, therefore, is no longer an issue, but discrimination is. I'm not referring here to the ability to discern good art from bad, but to distinguish something far more elemental and relevant. The humanities don't exist simply because we study them. The humanities—language, art, narrative, and philosophy—exist regardless. What the purposeful study of these forms can offer us at its highest level is a pathway to greater consciousness—greater *human* consciousness.

While art may be a valuable by-product of the study of the humanities, art is not its purpose. Art is a consequence of self-reflection. In his poem *An Essay on Man*, Alexander Pope invokes the Greek aphorism, "Know then thyself, presume not God to scan, the proper study of mankind is Man" (1994, 45).

It's easy to see that the humanities provide an essential portal into the study of man, but we tend to focus that study on its external form and activity, not on its internal function—to *know thyself.* We are inclined, therefore, to judge the arts, rather than to ingest them. And this neglect may be the real source of vulnerability for humanities programs. If the arts are viewed as merely the medium through which we make our existence more enjoyable, relatable, and tolerable, are we not inadvertently leaving them open to be *judged* as an expendable indulgence?

Encountering the arts in our culture has become such a passive and voyeuristic experience that we are often left without the use of their most vital function: to activate psychic development. Experiments with baby chimpanzees left in isolation indicate that they cannot thrive. We assume this is strictly because they need physical contact, but who's to say that their inability to develop isn't also a matter of having no example of how to live?

Were we to take a more holistic view of the humanities, we might see that language, art, literature, and philosophy conspire to reveal one, essential thing: *the human narrative.* Encoded in the language of every sonnet and every sitcom, every artistic masterpiece and every mundane mouthful of pop music is a part (no matter how minuscule) of the narrative that forms *the human instruction manual.* Perhaps, then, the great challenge, the real purpose, of the study of the humanities is to teach us how to read this manual, which consistently reveals that our problems are solvable, our trials are conquerable, and our wounds are healable.

"How shall I live?" isn't a mystery; the answer stares us in the face every morning when we arise with a new sun to its imagery of everlasting renewal. When one day dies, another is born. Hamlet didn't get this memo, but it's not too late for the rest of us. And, even if we don't "get" *Hamlet,* we may "get" Picasso's Blue Period, or Beethoven's 5th, or Lady Gaga's anthem "Born This Way."

I recently came across an interesting blog about the comic-book hero Superman and his vulnerability to kryptonite. Someone using the *nom de plume,* SupezM' wrote on killermovies.com: "His will keeps him going when his body wants to give up; willpower plays a huge factor in most of what he does. *What good is all the power in the world when you don't have the will to do anything?"* As far as I'm concerned, SupezM' just aced Humanities 101. He read the manual right; kryptonite wasn't Superman's greatest weakness; it was the potential source of his greatest strength. Our stories, as encoded in the manual, consistently reveal to us that our challenges are the source of our renewal because they beckon us to grow toward the fullness of our true nature—which *is* the source of our greatest strength.

When I was an undergraduate, I remember challenging one of my art history professors with the view that the image of Elvis painted on black velvet was as significant a work of art as anything hanging in the Louvre, depending on what it meant to a person. It was the 60's and I suspect I was just trying to be contrary. The professor called my bluff and had me write my term paper on the fine art of velvet painting. My initial response was to write something sassy and irreverent, but ultimately that just felt like I was proving his point. So I decided to take it more seriously and do some research. (Did you know that there was actually a museum of black velvet paintings in Portland, Oregon, called the Velveteria?!)

For three nights I sat in a dark corner of a local Mexican restaurant whose walls were adorned in all manner of velvet kitsch art. To be honest, I really had no idea what I was looking for, but I enjoyed sipping margaritas and munching nachos, trying to determine what effect, if any, these garish paintings had on people. Alas, I could find nothing that supported my wobbly little theory. For the most part the paintings were ignored or mocked, although, on one occasion, I did have the eerie feeling that Elvis's eyes followed me to the Ladies Room. But, then again, I'd been "sipping" lots of margaritas.

Only one incident held any potential. A group of drunken kids from the university got into a row and were dutifully thrown out, but not before one of their taco combination platters crashed to the floor. A busboy quickly cleaned up the mess; however, he didn't notice that a glop of guacamole had landed on the chin of a sad-eyed, velvet clown with a single rhinestone teardrop running down his cheek.

I kept vigil the rest of the night, hoping someone would care enough to rescue the clown from desecration. But it wasn't until closing that the same busboy happened to notice the offending green goo and unceremoniously wiped it off (actually, he rubbed it in).

I approached the young man, who told me his name was Javier, and asked what he thought of the painting. He responded with a shrug, which I glumly took as my cue to pack it in. But, just as I was preparing to leave, Javier stepped away from the painting to get a better look. He shrugged again, then added, "I guess, sometimes I feel like that, too."

Well, it wasn't much, but I came back the next day and took a photograph of the painting, which I then glued onto cardstock and underscored it with the quote from Javier. That was my term paper.

I got an "F."

My professor didn't get it, and I must admit that it took me another twenty years before I began to fully understand it myself. Javier's response to the clown image had little to do with the cliché that art is in the eye of the

156

beholder. Art is a product of the human psyche; it doesn't contain good or bad qualities; it just reflects our nature back to us in symbolic form, like images in a dream. In the corny rendering of the sad clown, a piece of Javier's own, true nature was affirmed. Does it really matter that the image was painted on black velvet? Does it make it less valuable—to him?

It is an unfortunate irony in the arts that intrinsic value seldom stands alone. Once art is deemed valuable, its worth becomes something to arbitrate. This relegates it to the status of property, which must be quantified and qualified in order to determine value. Inevitably, this leads to commodifying art. By making one image valuable and trivializing another, we risk losing our connection to the primary function of art—to carry unconscious information about the Self into the world.

This is not to say that we don't have the right to discriminate. Personally, the image of a clown on black velvet "creeps me out," and I definitely wouldn't want it hanging on the walls of my home. But I could say the same about the brilliant work of the late photographer Diane Arbus, whose candid portraits display the harsh reality of those we marginalize in our culture. Both exist, however, and by their very existence the nature of the world is revealed, if we choose to meet it on its own ground—which, sometimes, may be black velvet.

The other day, while standing in line at the supermarket, I noticed that the couple in front of me was laughing over a photo in a tabloid. It showed a man proudly holding up a pancake that he believed exhibited the image of Christ. It's easy to scoff at people who claim to see powerful iconic images on inanimate objects. But why is seeing Christ emblazoned on the face of a pancake any less meaningful to this man than seeing the image of his savior painted on the wall of the Sistine Chapel?

A thousand people may easily have gobbled down that same pancake without seeing anything. The fact that the image revealed itself to him and he recognized its numinous power means that he had something much more substantial to eat that day than fried dough and syrup. (In fact, I firmly believe that we should give bonus points to anyone who discovers an iconic image on their breakfast food!)

As Carl Jung described, "the treasure hard to find" is the goal or reward for the heroic journey to individuation. However, the path to that achievement is easily obscured unless we know how to read the road signs, which can include Jesus on a pancake. We'd like to think that our intellect, our faith, and our will to persevere are enough to get us to this holy land. But what we forget is that this destination, by its very nature, takes us into our own undiscovered regions. Therefore, we need the assistance of any road signs, maps, or instruction manuals that we can access.

Learning to engage the arts at this level should be *job one* of the humanities—to teach us how to *see through* the images that have emerged into the light of consciousness, and use them to illuminate the road ahead.

My humanities professor back in the 60's, and many more like him since, have been somewhat responsible for building obsolescence into this course by disregarding its most vital function—not to teach us how to merely see art, but how to see ourselves in it. Therefore, at this critical time in the evolution of the humanities, it is imperative to ask ourselves if we are, indeed, evolving. Sometimes our tenets, no matter how well intentioned, can become calcified and obdurate. What once held a vision of the bold new thing can easily become implacable dogma—if we don't respond to the call to change.

Early in my career as a script analyst and teacher in the field of screenwriting, I began to notice certain patterns in screenplays that indicated that there was a second, *internal* line of story structure that could be identified and replicated. Whereas the Aristotelian model aptly illustrates the exterior architecture of the dramatic narrative (the external conflict of the plot), this pattern I observed seemed to illustrate its interior counterpart (the internal conflict, or arc of the character). While there is no shortage of theoretical expositions on the topic and importance of internal conflict and the necessity for the arc of character in storytelling, I could find no source that actually addressed, with specificity, the particular pattern I was seeing.

Because I referenced these patterns in my work, I felt an obligation to resource and verify what I was teaching. I happened to have had access to a prominent professor in the field of literature, and she agreed to review my work. After we spoke for a while, she sat back thoughtfully, then said: "It's interesting, but who do you think you are to have anything new to say about classic story structure?"

In the moment, my reaction to that rebuke was to be contrite and apologetic. To be honest, at that time, I couldn't imagine that I *was* anyone who had anything new to say, which was why I felt the need to speak to her in the first place. But despite her admonishment, the patterns kept coming up for me, and fortunately I followed where they led—into the study of Depth and Archetypal Psychologies. Here I discovered that the patterns weren't new; they were as old as time itself, and the more I learned about them, the more I realized that they didn't just inform the nature of story— they held the key to our understanding of the universe itself. It was also the key to fully understanding and feeling confident about my own work—new or not.

Though I don't believe it was her intention, ultimately this literature professor did ask me the right question: *Who am I to have anything new to say?* It's taken me a long time find the answer, but eventually I did: *Who am I— who are any of us—not to have anything new to say?!*

I realize that the humanities professors I discuss here don't represent everyone who works in this field, but is the substance behind their attitude really so uncommon? If the humanities shelter themselves in such a rarified atmosphere that they hold no seat at the table for the most common among us, then whom do they serve? This was the nature of the question that Parsifal failed to ask the wounded Grail King when he had the opportunity. As a result Parsifal spent many years in the wilderness trying to regain access to that moment of glory. Does this have to be our fate as well?

The humanities may be wounded right now, but as Thomas Moore reminds us in his book *Care of the Soul:* "Soul enters life from below, through the cracks, finding an opening into life at the points where smooth functioning breaks down" (1994, 24)." Whether we like it or not, smooth functioning has broken down in the Humanities, and perhaps it's time to do a little *soul searching.*

Should all the humanities departments be shut down, only two outcomes are possible. If the bean counters are right, then we will live happily ever after without education in the arts and humanities; or, if they're wrong, creative resources will dry up and lead the culture back to the need (the "wantedness") for the study and understanding of our humanness.

In the meantime, let's check in with the human instructional manual for direction. If those indefatigable patterns hold true—which of course they will—the humanities will rise again. We can find proof of this in that chapter in the manual called "The Sun Always Rises." There we'll be reminded of the benefits achieved when the soil is turned, bringing nutrients to the surface that have too long been buried and neglected. And if that's not evidence enough, just read back through our own historical memory. The artistic urge has never been extinguished; in fact, it tends to thrive when it is forced to dig deep into the rich undergrowth of our very essence. It's hard to imagine a time in human history that was less hospitable to the arts than the Dark Ages and the ensuing centuries of Inquisitions. Yet, out of that miasma of human suffering and degradation came periods of reformation, romance, and renaissance.

Ultimately, Aristotle's view of literature is not the final word; Shakespeare's "to be or not to be?" is not the final question; and certainly, the closing of Humanities departments is not our final fate.

Art is the window to man's soul. Without it, he would never be able to see beyond his immediate world; nor could the world see the man within.
—Claudia "Lady Bird" Johnson

REFERENCES

Lennon, John. 1971. *Imagine*. LP. Apple, EMI.
Moore, Thomas. 1994. *Care of the Soul: A Guide for Cultivating Depth and Sacredness in Everyday Life*. New York: HarperCollins.
Pope, Alexander. 1994. *Essay on Man and Other Poems*. New York: Dover Publications.

PRACTICAL HUMANITIES: LIFE AND DEATH LESSONS FROM PROFESSOR SPHINX, AND YES, IT IS ROCKET SCIENCE

Barbara Mossberg, Ph.D.

These fragments I have shored against my ruins.
~T.S. Eliot, *The Wasteland*

To believe your own thought, to believe that what is true for you in your private heart is true for all men,—that is genius. Speak your latent conviction, and it shall be the universal sense.
~Ralph Waldo Emerson, *Self-Reliance*

When I was invited to contribute to this project on the case for humanities education I was with my eighty-nine-year-old mother who was dying, a word I no longer understood—something to do with life that was, yes, dying, but also, living vividly, living most profoundly—and unbearably. I began my professional career more than three decades ago in a tango with Tragedy 301 (Monday at 8:30 a.m.—in Oregon autumn mists). I am a poet and literary philosopher, teacher, dramatist, actor, dramaturg, scholar, consultant, and arts activist. It is my fortune to engage with the great minds tangling with terran wisdom. I have had positions with titles of Senior this and Distinguished that, president, dean. I have spoken around the world on how essential and improving the humanities are. Now here I was, in a life crisis—*my* life crisis: struggling to know what to do, what to feel, how I am called upon to act honorably, ethically, humanly. After all the scholarship, the learning, the devotion and discipline and practice, the teaching, the preaching—mine and a globes' worth of minds across earth, what have I got that is going to help me, and my mother, through this?

This is where the *rubber meets the road*. The role of the humanities? What is at stake in humanities education? Let's see. On the actual day I receive the call to reflect on humanities' import in civic life, my husband is receiving word on his latest medical tests following surgery, I have cowardly postponed a colonoscopy for the second time because of my brother's experience with his, my son is in Manhattan in a year's apartment lease, with no health insurance, with diabetes, and has just lost his job when his company was bought in an international merger, and my mother has not spoken to anyone in weeks, including me. On the phone with her the night before, I hear my words hurled into silence, no, the sound of breathing I cannot interpret. What is going on? Without our word exchange I am at a loss. What is the meaning? What is the story? I'm a literary critic specializing in the especially difficult, but I can't read this . . . this life.

In my mother's presence, I am equally illiterate. I have driven my weekly four hundred mile drive down to see her, and find her slumped in a wheelchair, head drooping to the side, eyes closed, her hands folded uselessly in her lap, shaking her head as a spoon is put to her lips. I fold her head into my arms. I pull a chair next to her, our knees touching, and take her hands in mine. I look into her face. She opens her eyes, looks back at me, and begins to utter. Sounds come from her throat, hoarse and whispery. They are the insides of words, without their shells. They are flowing sentences, currents of meaning, spoken earnestly. I cannot understand them. It is life itself to her to have me hear her, life itself to me to hear her, but I cannot, almost. Then just as difficult, or worse, some sounds form into words: . . . *help* (me). . . *I want . . . I want . . . I can't . . . I don't want . . .* followed by a helpless shrug.

Who can help me here? This humbling experience, fraught with despair; this comedy, right?—"The narrative". . . . in which I am the top-hatted dashing strutter slipping on a banana peel into the open man-hole—it's classic. . . the feisty fury of my mother, defiant, shrewd and busy and wise, who had to do everything for you, for herself, yanking down the steps and across the yard her own trashcans at eighty-six, while I'm an eye-rolling know-it-all slouch. The know-it-all presidency survivor, professor to doctoral leadership students, lecturer to medical and law schools and professional programs, consultant to organizations and boards, poetry performer—and clown—how is it I now feel so inadequate, reduced to shame, a helpless witness, by-stander to life's collapse?

At this moment when my ability to speak and read and comprehend seem irrelevant, when I am challenged in my core moral identity, struggling to understand what is happening to my mother and me, a meaning truer than medical and bureaucratic uselessness, my brain is scrolling and sweeping back and forth, left brain to right, some "what have we here" question, and finds lines by Yeats ("an aged man is but a paltry thing, a tattered coat upon a stick"), a passage from Donne ("ask not for whom the bell tolls . . ."), and suddenly the taunting unbearably true Beckett ("birth was the death of him"), and then T.S. Eliot ("shored these fragments against my ruins"), Emily Dickinson ("and I, and silence, some strange race, wrecked, solitary, here"), and Shakespeare ("that time of year thou mayst in me behold")—probably not accurate quotations but words alive in me planted who knows how many years ago. Beckett's lines flame up: "Where I am, I don't know, I'll never know, in the silence you don't know, you must go on, I can't go on, I'll go on." I realize that in this demoralized state, I am not alone, and perhaps this knowledge of what we all share, as I consider the usefulness of the humanities, is at the roots of what we need to live.

So I decide to make my criteria for assessing the humanities at the end of the day, how they serve me at this critical life and death moment. With the premise by Ralph Waldo Emerson, *"If you go into the deepest and most private and unique of your own experiences, you will speak for the man in the street, the maid with the pail,"* I will share with you, as I imagine you right now reading these words, learnings from my own journey that reflect on how humanities are practical and essential in our lives. I will return to my experience with my dying mother—how I was demoralized by my inability to understand what was happening and to change a single thing. The issue of the humanities being under question struck me powerfully, because throughout the whole ordeal with my mother—starting with my father's death and her stroke(s), then her fall(s), her losing language (perhaps)—the ability or desire to talk, to hear—dealing with state-of-the-art medical, technological, public policy, legal, and civic expertise, the one thing that got me—and my mother— through this life experience was, in fact, the humanities. I found the humanities essential even when, especially when, life is reduced to the unspeakable, the unspoken, the barely spoken, the hardly heard, the not understood, the not understandable. But because the humanities deal with the essential ways we are human, we may take their usefulness for granted, as a fish considers water.

Decades ago, as a young literature professor, I was asked to make the case for "the practical humanities" in public formats and settings to civic and labor leaders, as part of an initiative at the University of Oregon, to be responsive to a cultural-political climate in which the public was questioning the humanities' value as intrinsic to the core educational experience. In an increasingly technological world driven by economic realities, were the humanities irrelevant? Couldn't we do without them and save citizen time and money on what was really needed to learn? I framed my advocacy message with a recent *The New Yorker* cartoon in which a couple huddles in a doorway staring at a teenager writing cross-legged on the bed. One parent is turned to the other, saying, "Good news. It's economic theory, not a novel." The humanities were discredited as impractical, at the grassroots level of responsible parental love. Waving the humanities banner, I took issue with conventional wisdom that was not wisdom at all, arguing that economic theories come and go, whereas the novel expresses enduring truths of the human experience. I suggested that the parents' long term interests in their son's welfare could allow them to cheer a child's honoring humanities if they so fulfill him, rather than a choice of something he may not care about—but assumes is the practical path, heeding, *And no matter what you do, don't for goodness' sakes be an English major!*

The joke here from three decades later—this cartoon was published in the early1980s—first seemed to me to be how the joke is dated and could be reversed. Economic theories, in and out of fashion, are regularly and flamboyantly disgraced. Countries and regimes and economic empires and careers have collapsed on the fallen wings of failed theories. What does not change, what nothing can change, is the poignant human truth that parents care about and worry and suffer over their children's career choices. Deeper still: parents want their children to be happy. Parents want their children to be practical for the long run. Children are so often impractical (what do they know?). Our love makes fools of us, because we want to do the best we can for our children, but what do *we* know? It is so hard to be wise.

That's what I'm talking about, says the Sphinx to us, from thousands of years ago. When humanity is first evolving its ways of knowing, it makes symbols of what we have to say to each other, mental models. The image of the Sphinx in human history is one of our oldest symbols, and Sophocles invoked its message in his 5th century B.C. drama, *Oedipus the King.* Isn't it interesting that this model is a composite creature that walks four-footed on land, flies in the skies, and has the breasts of a woman? And isn't it interesting that this model speaks poetry? This ancient story has been the source of wisdom for people since the beginning of recorded time, including Freud's appropriation of the story to develop his science of psychology based on its enduring truths about human nature. What I ponder about this story is humanity's own understanding of what our most essential learning entails. The story goes that the city of Thebes is beset by a monster, the Sphinx, who serves as a one-chimera one-question entrance exam into the city. We can think of the Sphinx as a SAT exam, or Civil Service test. In order to enter Thebes, and be part of this community, one had to answer the Sphinx's test, a riddle: *what walks on four legs in the morning, two legs at noon, and three legs in the afternoon?* As the story goes, no one could answer the riddle, and one by one the applicants were choked ("throttled," hence the Sphinx's name as The Throttler) and hurled down the nearest cliff. Not knowing the answer to the riddle was a mortal sin, for which death was the only consequence. Enter Oedipus, trying to escape his oracled-fate of killing his father and marrying his mother (note to Freud: he didn't want to do that!), who answers correctly: "man." If the answer is the human being, the question is the mystery of the human experience, our sense of cognitive separation from whom and what we are. We are each living this life, aging every day, but we can't *see the forest for the trees*—and this expression is relevant, because the riddle is a metaphor from nature, a poem invoking human life as a journey like the day, subject to change by inevitable and harmonious and continuous cosmic processes. In the morning of our lives, as infants, we crawl on all fours. In mid-life, at the height of our powers, like sun at noon, we stride erect (albeit with Advil). As our powers wane, and we seek support from a cane (our "third leg"), we are like day's afternoon in the fading light.

In such real-world imagery, the human is defined by changes that are so transformational that people hearing this description cannot connect the three stages as belonging to the same entity—even if it is ourselves! The meaning of the riddle is how we humans change over time. But the meaning of the story of the riddle, it seems to me, is how hard it is to recognize our humanity when it comes in different forms and stages of behavior, as one continuous stream of development. To the ancient mind concocting this story, this moral lesson, we are imperiled without knowledge of connection, a vital understanding of human development that is the root of empathy and compassion based on our shared identical fates. Lacking such knowledge, we not only are not fit to live *with*, we are not fit to live *at all*.

But how is it, we might wonder, following this story to its logical source of reason, that people are represented as being unable to recognize human experience when it is laid out for them? Yes, the form of knowledge was wrapped in a metaphor, a poem. Wouldn't it be the fault, then, not of the people themselves, who could not answer the Sphinx, but of the educators of society, who did not provide this apparently life-saving literacy education? Couldn't the families of those heaved over the cliffs claim the City was liable for negligence in humanities education? To put a positive spin on this, we could argue that from a lawyer's point of view, consulting for the City, humanities education is critical to provide the populace. Humanities are an essential service. As William Carlos Williams said, in "To Asphodel, That

Greeny Flower," poems are "despised": "Look at/what passes for the new./You will not find it there but in despised poems./It is difficult/to get the news from poems/yet men die miserably every day/for lack/of what is found there."

But why does this essential wisdom without which we die, according to the ancient minds who created the story of the Sphinx and to Dr. Williams, who was an OB/GYN and dealt with life and death every day (so he should know), exist in a symbolic form of knowledge? Here we have a case of the mind seeking to create ways of making meaning, whether in stories of the past, as in history, or in interpretive arts, or in languages, and what is most confusing to me is how these forms of knowledge could be construed to be anything—besides difficult—but relevant or useful. Making our way in this world, with all we have to go on the evidence from our senses, trying to understand from patterns of rain and darkness, tree growth and sunlight, birth and death, how things work. It is all metaphor: $e=mc2$, or laws of motion, or the Brooklyn Bridge. At the core, engineering and mathematics and astronomy and architecture and music and poetry are indistinguishable. It is all about connection and relation. If we don't see these, we are alienated from each other and lack the spiritual wisdom we need to live.

The point I wish to make is that when we wish to be most practical, on behalf of those we love and honor, and offer career advice and educational options, we may think we are being practical when we pooh-pooh the humanities. But from the vantage of three decades later in the case of the economics theory cartoon, or three thousand years later, from the story of Oedipus and the Sphinx, some things don't change, and among those are human nature, and that is to say, the humanities. Perhaps the degree to which their value is obscured to us is the degree to which they are our mind's expressed self.

Putting on my educator's hat, I would say that the humanities deal with the deepest aspects of humanity, the expressive and philosophical arts. Although in evolutionary terms science and humanities were originally not divided but were inextricably woven as a fabric of knowing, it seems to me that they appear to the general public to be split along the lines of true and false, objective and subjective, orderly and disorderly, perfect and irregular. These divisions are not accurate and do not serve either sciences or humanities, nor do them justice, but the perception of sciences and professional knowledge as practical and no-nonsense, and humanities as a luxury (we can barely afford) is actually a danger to society's progression.

What links sciences, social sciences, humanities, and arts, is the integral right-left brain moral engagement of creativity in understanding how things

166

and beings are connected and interconnected, whether expressed in math as $2 + x = y$, or in poetry whether Emily Dickinson's "I'm Nobody," or Walt Whitman's *Leaves of Grass*": Do I contradict myself? /Very well, I contradict myself/I am large/I contain multitudes," or in physics as $e=mc2$, or in philosophy as *The Emancipation Proclamation* and the Preamble to *The Constitution,* "We hold these truths to be self-evident, that all men are created equal . . . ." Aristotle, Leonardo da Vinci, Thomas Jefferson, Emily Dickinson, Walt Whitman, Lincoln, Einstein, Gandhi, Martin Luther King, Richard Feynman, each expresses an urgency of conviction about the inextricable relation of arts, ethics, and social justice in time and space. If we probe discoveries and achievements in any field, we find humanities' roots. In *Chaos: Making the New Science,* James Gleick chronicles the development of chaos theory, an interpretation of whole complex systems out of emergent physics and mathematics, as based on the scientists' shared knowledge of literature and arts, whether nursery rhyme, Shakespeare, Wallace Stevens, Monet, Goethe, or Bach. The humanities expressed realities that scientists could integrate with theories—and a common language.

In fact, the humanities have always fostered developments in science thinking and social sciences. The humanities anticipate discoveries in fields hundreds and thousands of years later. Perhaps the public perception of humanities as not wholly practical comes from the idea that science takes up the general case, and humanities express the individual, idiosyncratic (if not eccentric), minority. Humanities deal with the creative realm and the uniqueness of each individual: we may be defined by systems ranging in scale and kind from cosmology to body mechanics to neurological bases of language, but we each use words and think thoughts and feel emotions and move in our own ways, that paradoxically stimulate us in turn to express these and thereby reveal a deep structure to humanity, what we all share in being human.

If we consider, then, as a wise society, what knowledge we should be providing ourselves as a species with which to go forward, it seems that the question ought to be what we need, based on what we have learned so far from our experience on earth. It is so clear to me that what we have learned includes the facts that social injustice destabilizes societies, that wars do not ensure peace, that inequity leads to social chaos, and that what the world needs now is love, sweet love. Love seems a namby pamby element to conclude a list of discoveries that have been identified as the most critical in thousands of years of human knowledge, but the message of love has been singled out not only by artists and writers and philosophers and humanists, but by Nobel-winning scientists, and by citizen leaders in civil and human rights. It turns out that "love is all there is" and other song lyrics express the same message as Einstein's in the aftermath of the atomic bomb. Einstein went from his studies at the Princeton Institute for Advanced Study to serve as advocate of humanities education and to speak on behalf of love, compassion, empathy, and peace.

If we are asking the question, what is the role of humanities education in civic enterprise, we can point to a peace advocacy of Einstein for evidence of the primacy of humanities in scientific thought—and what humanities' insights illuminate about human wisdom. But we can also look at outcomes, at how humanities education have changed the world and helped save the earth, by virtue of applying the meaning of love to civic culture. For example, we would not have our National Park System in the United States of America if it were not for humanities education. John Muir was raised on the poetry of the Bible, John Milton, William Wordsworth, Robert Burns, and Shakespeare (he had them memorized by the time he was a teenager). He took classes in history and literature, and geology and botany. When he saw a flower in a field, he "beheld" it; he "gazed" at it. He was filled with poetic rapture and inspiration. The way he understood nature was through the lens of the poets, and the poets' cadences informed the way he conceived and expressed wilderness to the scientific and civic leadership and general public. His writing was so different from conventional public policy advocacy that he touched the hearts of the public to the extent that national and state legislation protecting and preserving the wilderness came directly as a result of his writings. If we were to summon witnesses in defense of the practical value of the humanities, John Muir would be here to testify, arguing that preserving our forests is the most practical thing a person can do, and the way to preserve them is to make people "care about them" and "love them," as we do "our own children" and our elders. Muir would argue that it is through writing, writing in a way that integrates scientific reasoning, poetry, history, philosophy, and law, that we can invoke people's deepest and core humanity. In this way we save our own lives and that of the planet, and I am sure that Muir would correct me as I state this, saying that *our own lives* and that of *the planet* is a false and destructive differentiation as they are inextricably related. He would correct me with a poem—and an equation.

In similar ways, civil rights activists like Dr. Martin Luther King and Mahatmas Gandhi and Nelson Mandela would testify to the role of humanities in their own vision of what practical steps to take forward, their own courage and sense of mandate, and sense of historic community in which they operate. They would drag Henry David Thoreau to testify, and he would correct me right now by saying he might eschew society but he never lacked for courage in facing and challenging his fellow humanity to act ethically and morally, invoking . . . the poets, the philosophers, the humanities education that formed his own moral base.

We have an entire university curriculum of achievements and lives that testify to the essential role of humanities education, and access and exposure to humanities, to back up our claims of the humanities' practical value. What it comes down to is what is essential knowledge that we need to go forward in our lives. What is critical to know and do and understand? What is lifesaving literacy? What can't we do without, on this life journey? Our humanities have always been prophetic, from poetry to philosophy to history studies to science fiction, and yet there is another issue to consider in all the evidence before us. When the time comes for us to undergo an operation or be heard in a court of law, or dealt with by a claims adjuster, or thought of in a law regarding our retirement, or our children's options for education, or to go to war or end war, or be rehabilitated, who do we want making decisions and how do we want people to think of us? Is it not in our own most selfish interests to educate for qualities of empathy and compassion? That is, for "rocket science?" Here, I am struck by how the spheres of knowledge we think of as opposites, one imaginary, one real, one optional, one practical, are informed by minds which share an understanding of interdependence of all being—and hence human qualities of responsibility, ethics, integrity, and what we might call "moral genius."

And so I think now, taking off my educator's hat, and now with a "hat hair" (bad hair, flat hair), of my own story of what a humanities education has meant to me, in ways beyond my own career as a literary scholar and poet. I remember when I was a college president in a community going through a necessary transition to a more professional and business-like way of operating. It felt to many members of our community that its soul was being stripped from the college. I was responsible to diverse, conflicting constituencies, and the words of Walt Whitman would come to me about how he defined himself in terms of the nation, "large/I include multitudes." His vision of wholeness gave me a sense of common cause with all the dismayed people who find themselves on everybody's side even as no one gets along and or feels that the other belongs. Yet it was hard on my spirit. I spent days with lawyers and graphs and flow charts. I thought poetry had fled me forever. I would get comfort from watching a willow tree outside my window, whipped in wind, diminished before my eyes, but dancing, and one day, lines came to me, "my ballerina willow, in her tattered tutu." A metaphor! And through visions of dynamic complexity, I began to write poetry.

We hear the power of story, whether from a thousand years ago, *A Thousand and One Nights*, where stories saved both the life of Scheherazade and King Sharyar, the one who told and the one who heard, or the recent Tarsem Singh's film *The Fall*, with the same plot. Seeing my life as poetry was healing physically and spiritually to me and my community. Poetry became part of my formal and official and informal messages to the community, both my own and that of voices across the world. What helped me enormously was writing in my journal, and in that process, I was reminded of how writers across time had experienced a sense of responsibility and caring in an embattled world. I was reading history and biography in the mornings, and at one point I shared some of my journal with my Board of Trustees. My humble words, speaking truth to my experience and my own struggle to do right by this community, and seeing our struggles as part of a human struggle everywhere to find common cause and respect the precious creative spirit in each person, moved the Board in a way that legal memos and mission statements and graphs and charts did not. It opened up different ways of speaking to each other. We developed a new way of going forward. I found myself on the speaker's circuit on the topic of leadership and resilience. I had been in the news a lot, and people were surprised at how I found resources of energy and optimism for the daily work and the long road ahead. I would say that in the poetry and drama and stories that I have been privileged to read all my life, I felt nourished and even more importantly, a forgiveness and love of others and myself, for all of us, struggling on our paths to do the right thing, to belong, to matter, to be good.

And here is where I wish to conclude with what got me through my mother's death. It was the moral issue, of wanting to be good and to do the right thing for her and by her, and I did not know what that was. I could not say if she wished to live or die, in her straightened life. What could I do to help her, support her? What could help me in my own grief at the terrible sight and knowledge of my volatile fierce mother, tamed and maimed and constrained, unable to speak for and fight for herself when all her life she has fought for me and for justice and equal rights and compassion? Eleanor Roosevelt was her hero. I cannot say that I had a revelation or that it resolved in any heroic way. But what did happen was that I did the usual things with her. I said the poetry we had always said to each other, in person and on the phone and in letters. I quoted her favorite authors. And in this context, these poems came alive and are meaningful to me in new ways. My favorite poem that I recited for our college graduations and weddings (including my own) and Bar Mitzvahs and lectures is e.e. cummings's sonnet, "i thank You God for most this amazing." It has lines that read, "(i who have died am alive again today," and ends, "(now the ears of my ears are awake and/now the eyes of my eyes are opened)."

As I recited this poem for my mother (we used to say the words together), as she was in the process of dying, and *alive again today*, it seemed to me that in fact the poem was about not so much a birthday (the sun, life, wings, love) as re-birth. Of course! It was about resurrection, a day of new life for the liberation of the soul (it is not the trees that the poet sees, but the "spirits of trees"). I now saw that the poet had used the parentheses to suggest the interplay of life and death, the all-at-onceness of it as a totality, and that the poem was about the new life after death—waking up to paradise. Somehow, saying the poem gave me a new spirit with which to be with my mother, and help support her in her final weeks and days and hours. At the hour of her death, I was told by hospice to say my last words. This poem was my last set of words, after thanking her for the majesty of grace with which she had lived her life and loved us, with forgiveness, forbearance, and fortitude. Then the hospice nurse said, "She can yet hear: do you wish to say anything else?" At the moment in our lives when we are called on to use language and have it utterly matter, for all time . . . I remembered a poem I had written, thinking about her. It was in my computer. I clumsily jerked it up off the floor and read this poem from the screen:

Fat Lady Flying

Not the fence and not the ivy but it's you
Who's got to get lifted. No, no, you say,
It's not possible, I can't, and you are too full of despair.
Of course there are things that don't need to fly,
Things that are posted and rooted, nailed and nourished,
But you're not one of them.

With your life and your sentence of death
Which you share with frogs and the heron in the marsh
And the stars, and you see them soar and float,
Radiate and sing out in darkness,
You have to let yourself go.

You have seen elephants and the hippos swim,
Glide over river bottom,

You've seen the orangutan swing through the trees,
So you know the largeness of grace.

What I'm asking you to do now, don't look around,
It's you I mean, is to levitate. How?
Not by hoisting, not a case of heft, or heave,
Cranked by harness, this is not physics of motion.
I'm not sure but my guess is to breathe.

There's a way of holding breath
And it has to do with your eyes in this line,
Imagining the happiness of being weightless,
The buoyancy of a fat lady flying
Who doesn't even try, it comes when she laughs
And takes in the world, its splinters and pebbles,
Its cries and sagging truths, it's such a relief
The world exhales and she just rises.

That's you, how I see you,
See you flying, in these lines, your butterfly lungs,
Your head low, wind flows over and through you,
And what you hear now is your own voice,
Its awed silence, rising over the world.

When I wrote this poem, I was sitting at my desk, staring out the window, and feeling useless about my mother suffering, as I imagined, a lonely fate. Putting down words, engaging with the minds over time, I worked my brain seeking metaphors to express an understanding and in the process, discovered a community on earth sharing my mother's—and my—fate. In this moment of life and death, and new life, I felt the gift of the humanities as celebrating the human experience in its totality.

At the funeral parlor, I was asked to fill out the death certificate. On it was a space for my mother's occupation. She had been a bilingual educator in the East Los Angeles schools, and a supporter of civil rights, and a devoted mother and homemaker, a lover of nature, a gardener, an apostle of beauty, someone who loved earth and sky. What came to me to put was the highest praise I could give: "humanities educator." Her gift was the encouragement all my life to respect and pursue the humanities. She wanted me to be happy. In my encouragement of parents and civic leaders to ensure humanities education, I would say there is no more practical way to support "life, liberty, and the pursuit of happiness." Scholarship can document this across the disciplines, but it is with my own life experience, now at *three legs in the afternoon,* that I hear the Sphinx.

"To believe your own thought, to believe that what is true for you in your private heart is true for all men,—that is genius. Speak your latent conviction, and it shall be the universal sense" wrote Ralph Waldo Emerson. The saving thing about the humanities is how they address you in your hours of need and human frailties and hopes. It may not be genius, really, to cite your own experience and thoughts and in this way contribute to the whole, but leave it to the humanities to cheer us on, see the "us" in "genius," and encourage each person's voice as essential to what learning the community needs *now and forever* (and thank you, T.S. Eliot, for that phrase). The humanities ensure that on this human journey, we never walk alone.

REFERENCES AND FURTHER READING

Beckett, Samuel. 1978. *Collected Works of Samuel Beckett.* New York: Grove Press.

Buchwald, Diana Kormos, general ed. 1987–2009. *Collected Papers of Albert Einstein.* 12 vols. Princeton, N.J.: Princeton UP.

Calaprice, Alice, ed. 2005. *The New Quotable Einstein.* Foreword by Freeman Dyson. Princeton, N.J.: Princeton UP.

Carlin, John. 2009. *Invictus: Nelson Mandela and the Game That Made a Nation.* London: Penguin.

Cerf, Bennett E., ed. 1997. *The Arabian Nights' Entertainments or A Book of a Thousand Nights and a Night.* Trans. Sir Richard F. Burton. New York: Random House.

Churchill, Winston S. 1902/2005. *The River War: An Account of the Reconquest of the Sudan.* Alan Rodgers Books.

————.1941. *Blood, Sweat, and Tears.* Simon Publications.

————.1948. *The Gathering Storm.* Vol. 1 of *The Second World War.* New York: Houghton Mifflin.

————.2003. *Never Give In! The Best of Winston Churchill's Speeches.* Selected by Winston S. Churchill. New York: Hyperion.

cummings, e. e. 1994. "i thank You God for most this amazing." *Complete Poems, 1904-1962.* Revised, corrected, and expanded edition. Ed. George James Firmage. New York: Liveright Publishing Corporation.

Dickinson, Emily. 1999. "I felt a funeral in my brain." *The Poems of Emily Dickinson: Reading Edition.* Ed. R. W. Franklin. Boston: Harvard University Belknap Press.

————1999. "I'm nobody." *The Poems of Emily Dickinson: Reading Edition.* Ed. R. W. Franklin. Boston: Harvard University Belknap Press.

Donne, John. 2001. Meditation 17: "No Man Is an island." *The Complete Poetry and Selected Prose of John Donne.* Ed. Charles M. Coffin. New York: Modern Library.

Einstein, Albert. 1954. *Ideas and Opinions.* New York: Random House.

Eliot, T. S. 1991. "The Wasteland." In *Collected Poems, 1909-1962*. Boston: Harcourt Brace and Company.

Emerson, Ralph Waldo. 1837. "The American Scholar." Retrieved from http://www.emersoncentral.com/amscholar.htm.

———.1841. "Self Reliance." Retrieved from http://www.emersoncentral.com/selfreliance.htm.

Gandhi, Mohandas Karamchand. 1921/1982. "The Momentous Issue." *Collected Works of Mahatma Gandhi*. Vol. 25. New Delhi: Publications Division, Ministry of Information and Broadcasting, Government of India.

———. 1935/1976. "Letter to P. Kodanda Rao." *Collected Works of Mahatma Gandhi*. Vol. 67 New Delhi: Publications Division, Ministry of Information and Broadcasting, Government of India.

Gandhi, Rajmohan. 2006. *Gandhi: The Man, His People, and the Empire*. Berkeley: University of California Press.

Gangrade, K. D. 2004. "Role of Shanti Sainiks (Professionals) in the Global Race for Armaments." *Moral Lessons from Gandhi's Autobiography and Other Essays*. New Delhi: Concept Publishing Company. 154-55.

Gleick, James. 1987. *Chaos: Making the New Science*. New York: Penguin.

Green, Martin Burgess. 1986. *The Origins of Nonviolence: Tolstoy and Gandhi in Their Historical Settings*. University Park: Pennsylvania State UP.

King, Martin Luther, Jr. "Letter from a Birmingham Jail." Retrieved from http://www.africa.upenn.edu/Articles_Gen/Letter_Birmingham.html.

———.1998. *The Autobiography of Martin Luther King, Jr.* Ed. Clayborne Carson. New York: Warner Books.

Mossberg, Barbara. 2001. "Nature's Natural Ally." *Chaos Theory & Higher Education: Leadership, Planning, and Policy*. Ed. Marc Cutright. New York: Peter Lang Publishing. 203-49.

———. 2005. "John Muir's Beauty School, The Art and Science of Lifesaving Literacy." *Roots and Renewals: Writings by Bicentennial Fulbright Professors*. Ed. Mark Shakelton and Maarika Toivonen. Helsinki: Renvall Institute for Area and Cultural Studies, University of Helsinki.

———. 2007a. "How (and Why) To Save A Willow." *John Muir: Family, Friends, and Adventure*. Ed. Sally Miller and Daryl Morrison. Albuquerque: University of New Mexico Press.

———. 2007b. "If Trees Are Us: A Relativity Theory Showing the Genius of John Muir's Domestic Vision of Nature for Public Policy and the National Ethos for Civic Engagement." *John Muir: Family, Friends, and Adventure*. Ed. Sally Miller and Daryl Morrison. Albuquerque: University of New Mexico Press.

Murthy, B. Srinivasa, ed. 1987. *Mahatma Gandhi and Leo Tolstoy: Letters*. Long Beach, CA: Long Beach Publications.

Roosevelt, Eleanor. 1992. *The Autobiography of Eleanor Roosevelt*. New York: Da Capo Press.

———.2001. *My Day: The Best of Eleanor Roosevelt's Acclaimed Newspaper Columns, 1936–1962*. Ed. David Emblidge. Intro. Blanche Wiesen Cook. New York: Da Capo Press.

Shakespeare, William. 2004. Sonnett LXXIII. ("That time of year thou mayst in me behold"). *Love Poems & Sonnets of William Shakespeare*. New York: Doubleday.

Sophocles. 1996. *Oedipus the King. The Oedipus Plays of Sophocles: Oedipus the King; Oedipus at Colonus; Antigone*. Trans. Paul Roche. New York: Meridian.

Teale, Edwin Way, ed. 2001. *The Wilderness World of John Muir*. Boston: Mariner/Houghton Mifflin.

Tennyson, Alfred. 2000. Ulysses. *Alfred Tennyson: A Critical Edition of the Major Works*. Ed. Adam Roberts. Oxford: Oxford UP. 80.

Thoreau, Henry David. 1849/2009. *Civil Disobedience. The Thoreau Reader: Annotated Works of Henry David Thoreau*. Ed. Richard Lenat. Ames, IA: Thoreau Society. Retrieved from http://thoreau.eserver.org/civil.html

———. 1854a. "Slavery in Massachusetts." Ames, IA: Thoreau Society. Retrieved from http://thoreau.eserver.org/slavery.html.

———. 1854b/2009. Selections from *Walden. The Thoreau Reader: Annotated Works of Henry David Thoreau*. Ed. Richard Lenat. Ames, IA: Thoreau Society. Retrieved from http://thoreau.eserver.org/walden00.html

———. 1854c. Walden. Ames, IA: Thoreau Society. Retrieved from http://thoreau.eserver.org/walden00.html.

———. 1859. "A Plea for Captain John Brown." Ames, IA: Thoreau Society. Retrieved from http://thoreau.eserver.org/plea.html.

Williams, Carlos William. 1991. "Asphodel, That Greeny Flower." *The Collected Poems of William Carlos Williams, Vol. 1: 1909-1939*. Ed. A. Walton Litz and Christopher MacGowan. New York: New Directions.

Wordsworth, William. 1919. "Ode: Intimations of Immortality from Recollections of Early Childhood." *The Oxford Book of English Verse: 1250–1900*. Ed. Arthur Quiller-Couch. Oxford: Clarendon Press.

Yeats, W. B. 1996. "Sailing to Byzantium." *The Collected Poems of W. B. Yeats*. Ed. Richard Finneran. Revised 2nd ed. New York: Scribner Paperback.

CONTRIBUTOR BIOGRAPHIES

STEPHEN A. AIZENSTAT, PH.D. is a Clinical Psychologist and the Chancellor and Founding President of Pacifica Graduate Institute. His areas of emphasis include depth psychology, dream research and imaginal and archetypal psychology. Dr. Aizenstat has taught extensively at the K-12, undergraduate and graduate levels. His book, *Dream Tending*, describes applications of dreamwork in relation to health and healing, nightmares, the World's Dream, relationships, and the creative process. Dr. Aizenstat's methodologies extend traditional dream work to the vision of an animated world where living images in dream are experienced as embodied and originating in the psyche of Nature as well as that of persons. His other recent publications include: *Imagination & Medicine: The Future of Healing in an Age of Neuroscience* (co-editor with Robert Bosnak), "Dream Tending and Tending the World," in *Ecotherapy: Healing with Nature in Mind*; and "Soul-Centered Education: An Interview with Stephen Aizenstat" (with Nancy Treadway Galindo) in *Reimagining Education: Essays on Reviving the Soul of Learning* (co-edited by Dennis Patrick Slattery and Jennifer Leigh Selig).

KATHRYN LAFEVERS EVANS, THREE EAGLES, M.A. is a practitioner of Neoshamanic, or pantheist esoteric techniques and rituals since 1972, referring to her path as "reading the book of nature." She is a native Californian and Native American of the Chickasaw Nation, as well as of French heritage. Evans' academic research centers on the Renaissance Natural Magic of Jacques Lefèvre d'Étaples, tracing the lineage of C. G. Jung's *Red Book* to this tradition of the Florentine Platonic Academy. Her higher education degrees and training are in Literature and Writing, Research in Consciousness, Yoga, and esotericism in World Religions. Between 2002 and 2011, she presented academic papers on esoteric literature and Natural Magic at 13 conferences. A lifelong writer of nature and devotional poetry, Evans has performed in 12 cities.

NANCY GALINDO, PH.D. has worked as an educational consultant, community college instructor, seminar leader in public programs, and a small business owner. She holds an M.S. in Educational Psychology and a Ph.D. in Depth Psychology. Her teaching experience includes college courses in psychology and communication, and Ph.D. workshops in scholarly writing and active imagination. She is currently the Senior Admissions Counselor for the Ph.D. Program in Depth Psychology at Pacifica Graduate Institute. She leads women's groups, dream groups, and consults in private dream work. She has published: *Tending the Living Dream Image: A Phenomenological Study,* (2007); and "Soul Centered Education: An Interview with Stephen Aizenstat," (2009) in *Reimagining Education: Essays on Reviving the Soul of Learning.*

CYNTHIA ANNE HALE, PH.D., LCSW practices depth psychology as an educator, writer, researcher, and psychotherapist, exploring ways that inner and outer experience can be integrated through the creative imagination. She is a core faculty member at Pacifica Graduate Institute in California, where she teaches depth psychology and research as a transformative process in doctoral and master's degree programs. She also directs Institutional Research studies focused on educational effectiveness. Currently writing a book about the archetypal effects of empathically engaging with another person's experience of trauma, her work today is grounded in over twenty-five years as a psychotherapist. Her website is www.imaginalways.com.

DARA MARKS, PH.D. is a leading international script consultant, seminar leader, and the author of one of the top-selling books on screenwriting, *Inside Story: Power of the Transformational Arc. Creative Screenwriting Magazine* has consistently rated her the *best script consultant in the business* and she has worked in that capacity with many major movie studios and independent film companies. Marks received her doctorate in Mythological Studies from Pacifica Graduate Institute, focusing her dissertation on *The Transformative Function of Story.* Her continuing work in this field is devoted not only to deepening the craft of writing, but to moving modern storytelling into the realm of transformative art. Currently, she is writing a new book entitled *Engaging the Feminine Heroic,* which utilizes epic feminine mythologies as an archetypal guide into the soulful (Underworld) depths where the incorruptible connection to the essence of the human story can be recovered and given voice.

BARBARA MOSSBERG, PH.D. is a prizewinning humanities scholar, poet, professor, writer, actor, and public intellectual. She is President Emerita of Goddard College, Director and Professor of Integrated Studies at California State University Monterey Bay, and affiliated with graduate programs at Pacifica Graduate Institute and Union Institute & University in engaged humanities and ethical and creative leadership. Former U.S. Scholar in Residence for USIA/State Department, moderator and resource fellow for Aspen Institute for the Humanities, Senior Fellow at the American Council on Education, and Senior Fulbright Distinguished Lecturer, she lectures and consults internationally to inspire creativity, conscience, and courage for engaged civic culture: "learning for the whole self, the whole world, the whole life."

GINETTE PARIS, PH.D. is core faculty in the Mythological Studies Program at Pacifica Graduate Institute in Santa Barbara, California as well as Research Consultant in the Somatics Program. In addition, she is a psychologist, international lecturer and author of many books, among which is *Wisdom of the Psyche: Depth Psychology After Neuroscience* (Routledge, 2007). Her books have been translated into French, Spanish, Italian, Portuguese, German and Russian. Her latest book is *Heartbreak: Recovery from Lost Love and Mourning* (Mill City Press, 2011).

ROBERT ROMANYSHYN, PH.D. After six books, numerous articles and essays in edited volumes, Romanyshyn, who has been a clinical psychologist, psychotherapist, teacher and writer for 40 years, is now, finally (?), following the poet figure of his dreams out of the house of academia. Trying to begin again to be responsive to the elusive epiphanies of soul, he is working on a number of short volumes that at this juncture seem like essays in crafting an elemental psychology. His recently completed DVD, *Antarctica: Inner Journeys in the Outer World*, is part of this series, as is his recently completed book of poems, *Leaning Toward the Poet*. His DVD is available for viewing at www.jngplatform.com. His website is www.robertromanyshyn.com.

SAFRON ROSSI, PH.D. is Director of Opus Archives & Research Center, home of the manuscript and archival collections of scholars including Joseph Campbell and James Hillman. Safron is also Adjunct Faculty at Pacifica Graduate Institute, teaching courses on mythology and depth psychology. She earned her Ph.D. in Mythological Studies in 2009 and her writing and scholarly studies focus on archetypal psychology, feminist studies, and the western astrological tradition.

SUSAN ROWLAND, PH.D. is core faculty at Pacifica Graduate Institute, serving as Associate Chair for Hybrid Programs, and is formerly Professor of English and Jungian Studies at the University of Greenwich, UK. Her recent books include *Jung as a Writer* (2005), *C. G. Jung in the Humanities* (2010) and *The Ecocritical Psyche* (2011). Her work ranges from feminist critical theory to studies of novels, poetry, plays and film with a depth psychology perspective. She is also engaged with on myth and mystery fiction. From 2003-6, Susan was founding Chair of the International Association for Jungian Studies (IAJS) and in 2008 co-Chair of a joint IAJS-IAAP conference in Zurich.

JENNIFER LEIGH SELIG, PH.D. is proud to proclaim that she spent sixteen years teaching in a rural public high school before moving into various positions at Pacifica Graduate Institute, where she currently serves as Chair of Hybrid Programs, teaching and administrating in the Engaged Humanities and Creative Life Master's program and the Jungian and Archetypal Studies M.A./Ph.D. program. She has collaborated (conspired?) with Dennis Patrick Slattery previously, co-editing the book *Reimagining Education: Essays on Reviving the Soul of Learning*, and is the author of numerous essays and several books, including *Thinking Outside the Church: 110 Ways to Connect With Your Spiritual Nature*. Her website, including some of her essays and her photography, can be found at www.jenniferleighselig.com.

MICHAEL P. SIPIORA, PH.D. is currently a Core Faculty Member at Pacifica Graduate Institute. He was a professor at Duquesne University for over twenty years. Areas of Dr. Sipiora's teaching and publication include phenomenological psychology and philosophy, Archetypal psychology, and the rhetorical tradition. He earned a Bachelors and Masters in Philosophy at San Jose State University. His Master's and Doctoral studies in Psychology with a concentration in Literature were carried out at the University of Dallas. Sipiora is a licensed clinical psychologist who has practiced in both private and community mental health settings, and he has been active in narrative based, organizational development consulting.

DENNIS PATRICK SLATTERY, PH.D. is a core faculty member of the Mythological Studies Program at Pacifica Graduate Institute in Carpinteria, California. He is the author, co-author, editor or co-editor of 18 volumes, including four volumes of poetry, two with accompanying CDs. He is the author of over 300 essays that include a variety of scholarly, more popular cultural writings and book reviews that have appeared in collections,, magazines, journals and newspapers. He has offered Riting Retreats on exploring one's personal myth across the United States, Canada and Switzerland. He has been teaching for 42 years. www.dennispslattery.com

GWYN WOOD, M.A. continues her passion for film and travel to this day. She has worked in the film industry, the non-profit world and academia. She holds a Bachelor's degree in Film Studies and History, much to her parents' relief, and is completing graduate study in the Humanities. She currently works with the Engaged Humanities and the Creative Life and Mythological Studies graduate programs in Pacifica's Admissions office.

PAUL G. ZOLBROD, PH.D. is a native of Western Pennsylvania and Emeritus Professor of English at Allegheny College, where he served for thirty years. Zolbrod continues to teach by dividing his time between the Crownpoint, New Mexico Campus of the Navajo Nation's Diné College, New Mexico Highlands University, and Pacifica Graduate Institute. He earned the Ph.D. at the University of Pittsburgh, where he focused on late Medieval and early Renaissance literature. With a growing interest in oral influences on literary traditions, he turned to Native American mythmaking to learn more about that connection. Among other works, he is the author of *Diné Bahane': The Navajo Creation Story*, and *Battle Songs: A Story of the Korean War in Four Movements*.

www.ingramcontent.com/pod-product-compliance
Lightning Source LLC
Chambersburg PA
CBHW070349090426
42733CB00009B/1350